TOOLS FOR VALUING DIVERSITY

A Practical Guide To
Techniques For Capitalizing On Team Diversity

Anthony W. Harris

Selma G. Myers

San Francisco

Copyright © 1996 by Richard Chang Associates, Inc.

ISBN: 0-7879-5106-4

All rights reserved. No part of this publication, except those pages specifically marked "Reproducible Form," may be reproduced, stored in a retrieval system, or transmitted, in any form or by any means, electronic, mechanical, photocopying, recording, or otherwise, without the prior written permission of the publisher.

Printed in the United States of America

Published by

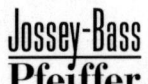

350 Sansome Street, 5th Floor
San Francisco, California 94104-1342
(415) 433-1740; Fax (415) 433-0499
(800) 274-4434; Fax (800) 569-0443

www.pfeiffer.com

Printing 10 9 8 7 6 5 4 3 2 1

ACKNOWLEDGMENTS

About The Authors

Anthony W. Harris, a consultant with Richard Chang Associates, Inc., is a highly-experienced human resource development practitioner who possesses diversified hands-on and management expertise in the areas of management development, employee relations, leadership development, organizational development, team development, and *"start-up"* of training and development systems.

Selma G. Myers, M.A., is president of Intercultural Development Inc., a California-based company specializing in diversity workshops, seminars and training for industrial companies, universities, financial institutions, utilities, health care firms, government departments, trade associations, and other organizations.

The authors would like to acknowledge the support of the entire team of professionals at Richard Chang Associates, Inc., for their contribution to the guidebook development process. In addition, special thanks are extended to the many client organizations who have helped to shape the practical ideas and proven methods shared in this guidebook.

Additional Credits

Editor:	Ruth Stingley
Reviewer:	Keith Kelly
Graphic Layout:	Christina Slater
Cover Design:	John Odam Design Associates

PREFACE

The 1990's have already presented individuals and organizations with some very difficult challenges to face and overcome. So who will have the advantage as we move toward the year 2000 and beyond?

The advantage will belong to those with a commitment to continuous learning. Whether on an individual basis or as an entire organization, one key ingredient to building a continuous learning environment is *The Practical Guidebook Collection* brought to you by the Publications Division of Richard Chang Associates, Inc.

After understanding the future *"learning needs"* expressed by our clients and other potential customers, we are pleased to publish *The Practical Guidebook Collection*. These guidebooks are designed to provide you with proven, *"real-world"* tips, tools, and techniques—on a wide range of subjects—that you can apply in the workplace and/or on a personal level immediately.

Once you've had a chance to benefit from *The Practical Guidebook Collection*, please share your feedback with us. We've included a brief *Evaluation and Feedback Form* at the end of the guidebook that you can fax to us at (714) 727-7007.

With your feedback, we can continuously improve the resources we are providing through the Publications Division of Richard Chang Associates, Inc.

Wishing you successful reading,

Richard Y. Chang
President and CEO
Richard Chang Associates, Inc.

TABLE OF CONTENTS

1. Introduction 1
Why Read This Guidebook?
Who Should Read This Guidebook?
When And How To Use It

2. Understanding Workplace Diversity 7
The Meaning Of Culture
The Influence Of Stereotypes
The Predicament Of Prejudice
The Importance Of Valuing Diversity

3. First Impressions 13
Why Use "First Impressions"
When To Use "First Impressions"
How To Use "First Impressions"
Reinforcing The Lessons Learned

4. Gender Scripts 23
Why Use "Gender Scripts"
When To Use "Gender Scripts"
How To Use "Gender Scripts"
Reinforcing The Lessons Learned

5. Diversity-Based Team Building 37
Why Use "Diversity-Based Team Building"
When To Use "Diversity-Based Team Building"
How To Use "Diversity-Based Team Building"
Reinforcing The Lessons Learned

6. Nonverbal Exchanges 49
Why Use "Nonverbal Exchanges"
When To Use "Nonverbal Exchanges"
How To Use "Nonverbal Exchanges"
Reinforcing The Lessons Learned

7. Communicating Interculturally 61
Why Use "Communicating Interculturally"
When To Use "Communicating Interculturally"
How To Use "Communicating Interculturally"
Reinforcing The Lessons Learned

8. Listening Competency 71
Why Use "Listening Competency"
When To Use "Listening Competency"
How To Use "Listening Competency"
Reinforcing The Lessons Learned

9. Diversity-Based Conflict Resolution 81
Why Use "Diversity-Based Conflict Resolution"
When To Use "Diversity-Based Conflict Resolution"
How To Use "Diversity-Based Conflict Resolution"
Reinforcing The Lessons Learned

10. Cross-Cultural Coaching 93
Why Use "Cross-Cultural Coaching"
When To Use "Cross-Cultural Coaching"
How To Use "Cross-Cultural Coaching"
Reinforcing The Lessons Learned

11. Summary 105

Appendix:
Reproducible Forms And Worksheets 107

"The time has come to step off the road and cut a brand new path."

Maya Angelou

CHAPTER ONE

INTRODUCTION

In today's business world, workplace diversity is a hot topic. And its significance increases proportionately as the work force becomes more and more diverse; that is, it includes differences in gender, age, ability, sexual orientation, race, and ethnicity. Workplace diversity can either cause ruptures in the fabric of an organization; or, if handled correctly, it can be woven into strong fibers to support that same organization.

Valuing diversity is the key. It's the valuing of employees and their differences that allows an organization to develop broader perspectives and to approach business problems in new and creative ways.

Whether in or out of the workplace, the ability to learn from people regarded as different is instrumental to the process of becoming fully empowered. When we learn to pay attention to people as unique individuals, while also recognizing and taking into account their differences as members of particular groups, they feel valued. And valued employees quickly become one of an organization's greatest assets.

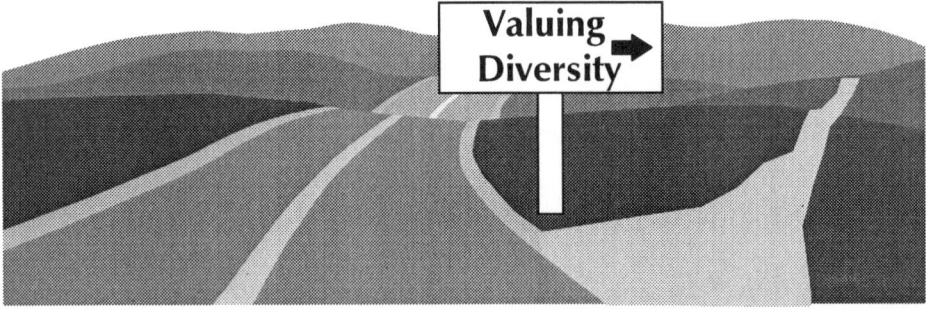

Workplace conformity belongs to a past era. So take the challenge to value diversity and use it to your advantage in your organization.

TOOLS FOR VALUING DIVERSITY

INTRODUCTION

Why Read This Guidebook?

Today's work force includes people from various ethnic groups, cultures, races, genders, ages, religious backgrounds, sexual orientations, and abilities. If you want to increase communication and teamwork among them, the tools in this guidebook will be invaluable. The tools will help prevent worker alienation and encourage better understanding of the differences among people.

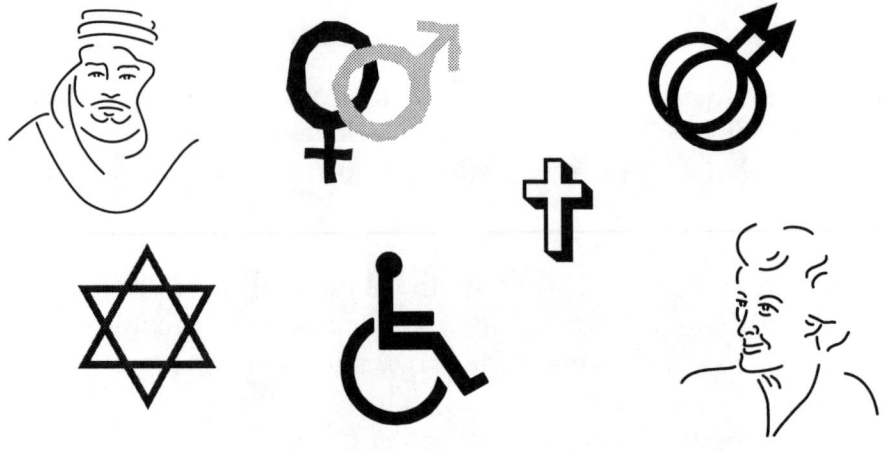

Differences among people sometimes create discomfort and conflict. Managers and leaders in the workplace face critical challenges in finding the most effective way to help people deal with differences. This guidebook will help improve harmony, productivity, and comfort by providing an understanding of the motivations and perspectives of others.

In today's diverse global business environment, being able to interact effectively with people different from ourselves is a necessity for leaders, managers, and individual employees in every organization.

INTRODUCTION

Who Should Read This Guidebook?

This guidebook is a must for managers, team leaders, supervisors, coaches, facilitators, and trainers who need to use tools and team exercises to increase staff awareness and skills in a diverse workplace. If you are a member of a team who needs to learn, or would like to help others learn how to appreciate and understand workplace diversity, you should read this guidebook. It can also be read as a self-study reference to assist any individual in dealing with people in all situations.

When And How To Use It

Use this guidebook whenever there is a need to conduct team-building sessions, to deal with interpersonal problems among people in the workplace, to resolve communication issues, and to manage conflicts on the job.

Do you desire to help others understand and appreciate the diversity that exists in today's workplace? Use the tools contained in this guidebook. They'll prove invaluable when giving and receiving feedback, when preparing teams to conduct data collection, when problem solving, when helping your team develop and complete tasks and goals, and even when identifying your own management and leadership style.

INTRODUCTION

In addition, review the eight tools presented in this guidebook every time you have to conduct a team-building activity, increase interpersonal communication skills, improve people's negotiation skills, or deal with conflicts within your team. Make sure your team members have their own reference copy. It's a *"must-read"* for them also.

For further reading and training application material on the topic of workplace diversity, please see the entire Workplace Diversity Series of guidebooks *(five titles)* of which this book is part. The lead or *"parent"* guidebook in the series, *Capitalizing On Workplace Diversity*, presents an overall approach and model for an organization or work group to succeed with its diversity as one of its core strengths.

One element of this overall model, building workforce capability, is expanded upon in detail in the other three guidebooks in the series, *Successful Staffing In A Diverse Workplace, Team Building For Diverse Work Groups,* and *Communicating In A Diverse Workplace.* Each of these guidebooks presents a platform from which employees can improve the skills and further develop the competencies needed to contribute to the success of a diverse organization. The guidebooks can be used individually *(in a self-study environment)*, or they can be used in a facilitated group setting, as is the case with *Tools For Valuing Diversity*.

Tools For Valuing Diversity provides more than a token attempt to understand people's differences. It is a guide that allows individuals to delve within themselves, to observe, to discuss, and to emerge as partners willing to use diversity to increase the effectiveness of their organization. Valuing diversity is definitely a challenge, but it's also one challenge worth attempting.

INTRODUCTION

The Organizational Diversity Success Model™

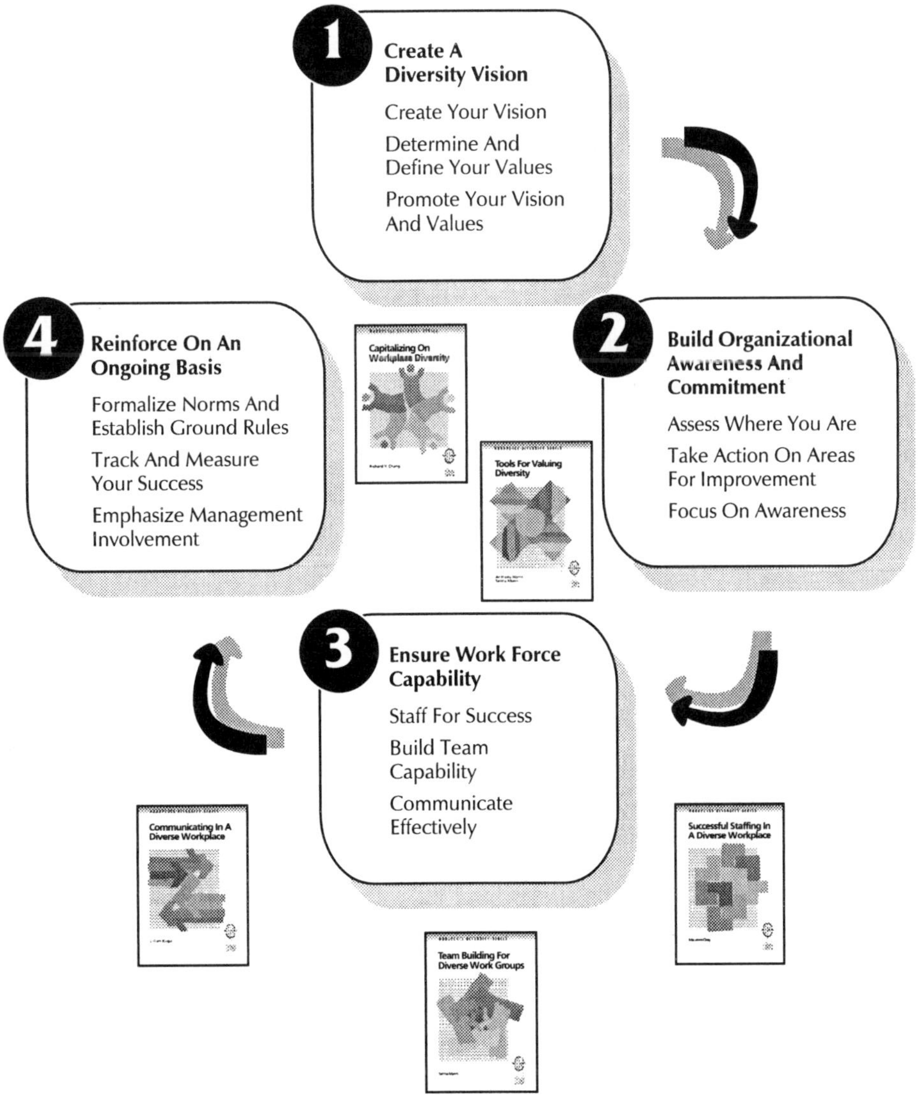

① Create A Diversity Vision
- Create Your Vision
- Determine And Define Your Values
- Promote Your Vision And Values

④ Reinforce On An Ongoing Basis
- Formalize Norms And Establish Ground Rules
- Track And Measure Your Success
- Emphasize Management Involvement

② Build Organizational Awareness And Commitment
- Assess Where You Are
- Take Action On Areas For Improvement
- Focus On Awareness

③ Ensure Work Force Capability
- Staff For Success
- Build Team Capability
- Communicate Effectively

CHAPTER TWO

UNDERSTANDING WORKPLACE DIVERSITY

As the business environment becomes more global and the work force becomes increasingly more diverse, valuing workplace diversity shoots to the top as a critical issue for today's organizations. White, English-speaking, American-born males aren't the only people in the workplace. That's been clear for quite a while. But we have more to consider than people of different ethnic groups, gender, culture, and language. We also have to learn to deal effectively with people of different ages, abilities, religious backgrounds, and sexual orientations.

To better understand the importance of valuing workplace diversity and how the tools in this guidebook can help accomplish that goal, let's look at some common definitions and terms commonly used in discussing workplace diversity.

The Meaning Of Culture

The *Concise Columbia Encyclopedia* defines culture as *"a way of life of a given society, passed down from one generation to the next through learning and experience."* If you consider this definition, it becomes clear that culture goes deeper than one might think. Culture is complex.

Culture impacts every aspect of life, from the way people behave toward one another to their relationship with the natural environment. It includes beliefs and values, as well as assumptions and perceptions. People's behaviors often stem from their culture and its values. For example, some cultures value harmony and balance and believe in saving face. Fear of embarrassment or humiliation would be of great concern to a worker with that ethnic background and could manifest itself in workplace behaviors such as a hesitation to take the initiative or to try out a new procedure.

UNDERSTANDING DIVERSITY

It is quite easy to see how cultural clashes could occur in the workplace. The more you know and understand about your own and others' cultures, the better you can address the issues that arise. In dealing with the worker who stalls when he should be using a new procedure, you might explain that Americans value taking the initiative and that you promise not to get upset if he makes mistakes. The more you understand the influence of culture, the more effective communication can be.

The Influence Of Stereotypes

Stereotypes are defined as fixed, inflexible notions about a group. Stereotypes, whether positive or negative, are the heart of prejudice. They block the ability to think about people as individuals. Many stereotypical generalizations are based on misconceptions and errors in judgment.

Sometimes people generalize too much or stereotype simply because they do not have the facts, have limited personal experience, or are working with distorted information. For example, a manager may unwittingly bypass older employees for special projects in her department, because she views older people as she views her own parents—more set in their ways, less creative, and too tired to take on additional work. Her limited personal experience leads her to stereotype her employees and does a disservice to both her organization and the employees.

We first must learn to identify the stereotypical perceptions we hold, then work toward changing them. The manager in the previous paragraph may decide to offer a special project to an older employee if she, by herself or with help, identifies the stereotypes she holds and learns to let go of them.

The Predicament Of Prejudice

Prejudice involves an unreasonable bias or an opinion formed before the facts are known. Prejudice, often negative, causes suspicion and intolerance, and frequently brings out irrational behavior. It can easily damage interpersonal relations and cause communication breakdown.

An example of prejudice is homophobia. Workers who consider homosexuals to be unworthy individuals will not work well nor communicate well with them. Such prejudice negatively affects not only the individuals involved, but also the organization. Teamwork suffers as communication lines disintegrate.

It is important to recognize prejudices and not let them get in the way of building team relationships across cultures. People who recognize them for what they are have taken the first step towards overcoming them. It may take longer to overcome certain prejudices, but it can be done.

The Importance Of Valuing Diversity

Valuing diversity is a way of helping people deal with issues created by their differences. As people learn to focus on the value of differences, they become open to learning from people they regard as different. This also helps them build empowered relationships in which they work together as true team members.

Culture, stereotypes, and prejudice complicate workplace issues. Whether you are a manager, team leader, supervisor, or team member, you face many obstacles in dealing with diversity issues. By using the tools in the chapters that follow, you will be able to minimize obstacles and capitalize on any group's diversity. You will have an opportunity to expand *"self-awareness,"* understand others more clearly, build skills, and develop techniques that you can incorporate into your team ground rules or norms. Let workplace diversity work for you by learning to value it!

CHAPTER TWO WORKSHEET: HOW DIVERSE IS YOUR WORKPLACE?

1. Describe the nature of diversity within your workplace.

_____

_____

_____

_____

_____

_____

_____

2. Give an example of a cultural clash in your organization.

_____

_____

_____

_____

_____

_____

_____

UNDERSTANDING DIVERSITY

3. List examples of stereotypes and/or prejudice in your organization.

_____
_____
_____
_____
_____
_____
_____
_____

4. On a scale of 1 to 10, with 1 being low and 10 being high, how would you rate your organization's commitment to valuing diversity? Why did you choose that rating?

_____
_____
_____
_____
_____
_____
_____

CHAPTER THREE

FIRST IMPRESSIONS

When someone mentions the name of a group of people, your first thoughts of that group reflect the opinions you hold about them. And those first thoughts, whether positive or negative, are usually stereotypes. This *"First Impressions"* activity can be used as a tool to help members of your team or group examine the stereotypes associated with the groups of people with whom they interact.

Why Use *"First Impressions"*

Stereotyping is unfair and often becomes a barrier to good communication and acceptance of people as individuals. Whether they realize it or not, everyone stereotypes. For individuals, partners, or teams to work effectively with others, they must be aware that they do stereotype others. Then, they must learn to disregard the stereotypes and accept individual differences. Awareness of stereotyping is the first step toward eliminating it; *"First Impressions"* brings that awareness into the open.

When To Use *"First Impressions"*

Use *"First Impressions"* as a tool whenever you want to:

- Increase interpersonal skills and build effective communication skills within your work group.

- Help teams, work groups, and individuals examine the stereotypes associated with the groups of people with whom they interact.

- Assist your team members in recognizing that stereotyping is unfair, and that it contributes to communication problems.

- Encourage the members of your group to accept people as individuals.

FIRST IMPRESSIONS

Rob, an electronics store manager...
was having difficulty with his stereo installation group appreciating each other's cultural and ethnic backgrounds. Rob decided to use the *"First Impressions"* tool during an upcoming staff meeting. He thought that if he could get all of the group members *(Arvella, Scott, Raul, Maria, Malika, Charles, Yolanda, Franco, and Debra)* to better understand how stereotypes lead to division, then the group might become a stronger and more productive team....

How To Use *"First Impressions"*

Whether you use this tool with your team or with other individuals, complete the following four steps:

Step 1: Start the *"First Impressions"* session

Step 2: Brainstorm adjectives and divide list into two categories

Step 3: Break into small discussion groups

Step 4: Review key definitions

Step 1: Start the *"First Impressions"* session

First, set a time limit for the session. Generally, forty to sixty minutes is sufficient. Next, describe the agenda for the session to your team, so they are aware of what will be taking place. For *"First Impressions"* to work effectively, the team must agree that by the end of the session they will come up with a plan to reinforce the lessons learned.

Finally, prepare or hand out any items necessary for the session. In this case, you need to provide each individual with paper and a pencil or pen, and you must have a *"First Impressions"* list, composed of the names of different groups of people. *(Use the list on page 20, and add or delete, as appropriate.)* Either hand out a separate list to each team member or use a flip chart. Ensure that your writing is large and legible enough for all to read.

FIRST IMPRESSIONS

Rob spent a few minutes...

describing *"First Impressions"* to his stereo installation group. *"Stereotypes are natural,"* he said, *"but they're often destructive, because they don't take into account the individual."* The group seemed receptive and agreed to work together on a plan of action at the end of the session. Rob ended by handing out pencils and paper to each person and showing the group the list of words he had written on a flip chart....

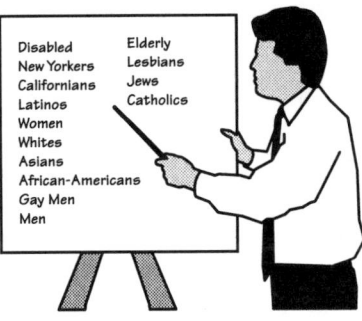

Step 2: Brainstorm adjectives and divide list into two categories

This step consists of two separate tasks each individual will do independently. You will ask the members of your team or group to write the first two or three adjectives that comes to mind for each of the groups listed. Stress that they are to write their first thoughts, whether positive or negative.

FIRST IMPRESSIONS

Disabled: limited, courageous

New Yorkers: abrasive, unfriendly

Californians: hurried, fun-loving

Latinos: romantic, unmotivated

Women: sensitive, indecisive

Whites: ambitious, spoiled

Asians: intelligent, quiet

African-Americans: athletic, simplistic

Gay Men: feminine, sensitive

Men: strong, violent

Elderly: frail, exploited, knowledgeable

Lesbians: masculine, harsh

Jews: frugal, loud

Catholics: devout, unchanging

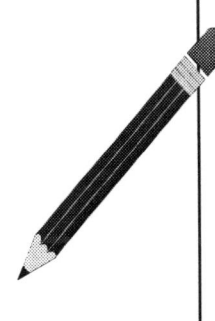

FIRST IMPRESSIONS

Then ask each individual to divide the list into two categories—easy and difficult. Which of the groups were easy to describe? Which of the groups were more difficult to characterize?

> ### Rob asked his team...
> to jot down the first two or three positive or negative adjectives that came to mind. *"Take ten minutes to list the adjectives,"* he said. The members of the group started writing. By the end of eight minutes, it looked as if most of the team members had stopped writing. Rob asked the group to take a minute to look at their individual responses. *"Next, I'd like you to divide the list into two categories—easy and difficult. Put an 'E' by the groups that were easy to describe and a 'D' by those that were difficult."...*

Step 3: Break into small discussion groups

Divide your team into groups of three and give them fifteen to twenty minutes to discuss their reactions to the activity and to stereotyping in general. Have them also discuss why certain groups were easier to characterize than others.

> ### When everyone was finished categorizing...
> the adjectives, Rob split them into three groups of three members each. *"Take twenty minutes to discuss your responses and your categories,"* he said. *"And don't forget to include stereotyping in your discussion, because that's what we do when we generalize."* Rob walked around the room, listening to the discussions. He heard both positive and negative adjectives. *"I don't usually think about the disabled,"* Raul commented. *"But I did come up with 'aggressive,' because I always see them on television seeking special treatment."* Debra disagreed. *"That wasn't my response at all,"* she said. *"I think they're courageous for all they have to overcome."* Rob let the groups continue to share their examples with each other....

FIRST IMPRESSIONS

Step 4: Review key definitions

The *"First Impressions"* tool hits home when participants realize that stereotypes and prejudice influence them much more than they previously thought. After the small discussion groups finish, lead the entire group in a discussion which reviews and reinforces the following definitions of *"stereotype"* and *"prejudice."*

A stereotype is defined as an exaggerated belief or fixed idea about a person or group that is held by people and sustained by selective perception and selective forgetting. Stereotypes are natural, but they are often destructive because they are unfair, they do not allow for individuality, and they interfere with communication.

Stereotypes come from:

- Incomplete, distorted information and limited personal experience
- Outside sources such as others' interpretations of cultural behavior

Prejudice is defined as a preconceived idea or negative attitude, formed before the facts are known and sustained by over-generalizations. Prejudice usually resists all evidence. It implies inferiority, leads to suspicion, and is detrimental to communication and interpersonal relations. The tendency is that people who reject one out-group will also reject other out-groups.

Rob reviewed...

the two key definitions and their sources. The group agreed that they made many more stereotypical judgments and prejudicial statements than they thought they did. Yolanda spoke up. *"Our adjectives were all based on generalizations,"* she began. *"And no one likes to be described or judged on those terms."* Raul agreed. *"I don't like people thinking I'm part of a gang just because I'm Hispanic,"* he said. *"That's prejudice!"* The group continued their discussion....

FIRST IMPRESSIONS

Reinforcing The Lessons Learned

What lessons have you learned from this activity? A tool is only effective in the hands of a willing user. *"First Impressions"* is more than an exercise in responses. It's designed to help you and your team delve into the reality of stereotyping and prejudice, and emerge with a realistic way to counteract their destructiveness.

Lessons learned

With your team or group, list the lessons you've learned. Then work together to create a plan that will keep those lessons vivid in your minds.

Rob asked the team...
to come up with a list of lessons they had learned and to then create a plan of action for helping them overcome their stereotypes and prejudice of people. It didn't take the group long to list a few lessons they had learned.

LESSONS LEARNED

1. Recognize that we all stereotype and are all prejudiced to some degree.

2. We are quick to stereotype and pre-judge others.

3. Stereotypes and prejudices influence our judgment and alter our communication with others.

FIRST IMPRESSIONS

"Those are good lessons to learn," Rob said. *"Having learned them, then, how can we act differently?"* Malika answered with, *"I know. Since the first step involves awareness, we need to make sure we are always aware of the fact that we do stereotype."*

Arvella stepped in. *"And since we're quick to stereotype, maybe we need to learn to wait before we respond to people." "Good point,"* Scott said. *"If we wait, then we can take the time to separate facts from stereotypical responses."* The group continued discussing, until Rob interrupted. *"You all have given valid ideas for individual ways to keep us from stereotyping others. Now, how can we make sure we continue doing what we've said?"*...

Create an action plan

Once you've agreed on what lessons you have learned from *"First Impressions,"* work with your team or group to create a plan that will help reinforce those lessons.

Debra responded ...

"I am willing to organize some 'brown-bag' lunch sessions on understanding people's differences. We can also discuss our individual attempts to counteract stereotyping." Charles jumped in. *"And we can look into getting other resources for our team to read and study,"* he said. *"I'd be willing to do that."* The team agreed on the action plan.

"First Impressions" is a tool to start individuals thinking about diversity in different terms. Once people can get past stereotyping, they're able to look at others more realistically, and they begin seeing others as individuals, not as representatives of a group. The challenge has just begun!

First Impressions

Look at each of the words below and write down just the first two or three adjectives that come to mind—your thoughts or traditional stereotypes—positive or negative.

Disabled:
New Yorkers:
Californians:
Latinos:
Women:
Whites:
Asians:
African-Americans:
Gay Men:
Men:
Elderly:
Lesbians:
Jews:
Catholics:

Chapter Three Worksheet: Recognizing Stereotyping

1. Use *"First Impressions"* with your team or group. What are the key lessons learned and what will your team do differently in the future?

2. List other specific teams in your organization which would benefit from using the *"First Impressions"* tool.

3. Choose one of the teams you listed in number two and list the group names you would want that team to describe.

CHAPTER FOUR

GENDER SCRIPTS

Diversity exists, in part, because we draw on our own life experiences. Our experiences, both long past and recent, color our perceptions of ourselves and others. Early experiences often greatly influence how we relate to and perceive those of our own sex, as well as those of the opposite sex.

Why Use *"Gender Scripts"*

The term *"Gender Scripts"* refers to the way people's attitudes, perceptions, assumptions, and expectations have been formed in earlier years, specifically about gender. They have been imprinted, either through personal experiences or external influences. Old programming is hard to erase, and many of the problems that occur between men and women in the workplace relate back to early experiences. Awareness of the *"programming"* is key to getting rid of erroneous perceptions.

When To Use *"Gender Scripts"*

"Gender Scripts" can be used as both a preventive *("before-the-fact")* and a prescriptive *("after-the-fact")* tool. Use as a preventive tool when:

- No major problems have occurred in your organization, but the odds are that gender issues will surface at some point.

- A change has occurred in your organization that makes it a relevant topic (e.g., a new hire makes a number of unwelcome comments, one sex has a much greater percentage of recent promotions, etc.).

GENDER SCRIPTS

Use as a prescriptive tool when:

- ♦ It's evident gender issues have cropped up (e.g., an employee has complained, you've noticed difficulties, etc.).
- ♦ Someone has been reprimanded or fired because of gender issues. (Employees may be wary of falling into the same situation, but that will pass with time. The problem may not be solved.)

Johanna, the Director of Financial Analysis/Planning...

was aware of general dissatisfaction in her department. It was nearing budget time, so workloads were increasing. Some of the female financial analysts felt that the male analysts were taking unfair advantage of them, dumping additional menial tasks into their laps. Johanna called a meeting to use the *"Gender Scripts"* tool....

How To Use *"Gender Scripts"*

"Gender Scripts" can be used individually, in teams, or with others of your choice. If you use this tool with others, complete the following five steps:

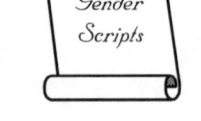

Step 1: Start the *"Gender Scripts"* session

Step 2: Complete Worksheet #1 and divide into discussion pairs

Step 3: Reconvene as a group and discuss

Step 4: Complete Worksheet #2, Part I; then discuss Part II with same partner

Step 5: Reconvene as a group and discuss

Step 1: Start the *"Gender Scripts"* session

Set a time limit for your *"Gender Scripts"* session. Fifty to sixty-five minutes generally is sufficient for this exercise. Describe to your team members what will take place during the session and gain acceptance for creating a plan to reinforce the lessons learned.

GENDER SCRIPTS

Participants should use the worksheets provided in this chapter. Also provide pencils or pens for each individual.

> ### *A few of the department members...*
> balked when they heard a meeting was scheduled. *"Don't we have enough to do?"* Curtis, one analyst, asked. When Johanna explained that the purpose of the meeting was to relieve some of the tension and take care of some problems, he quieted down.
>
> At the meeting, Johanna described in greater detail the contents of the session and asked if all would agree to creating a plan at the end of the session. All seven (*Curtis, Pauline, Gretchen, Alek, Raymond, Karen, and Marcelina*) nodded....

Step 2: Complete Worksheet #1 and divide into discussion pairs

Have participants complete Worksheet #1. Allow about five minutes for this task. Ask group members to be fairly brief. They can elaborate on their responses when they discuss them with their partners.

Group the members of your session into pairs and have them use the completed worksheet as a discussion guide. If the number of participants is uneven, use yourself as the additional person. Allow ten to fifteen minutes for the pairs to discuss their responses with each other.

> ### *Johanna directed the group to Worksheet #1...*
> and instructed the group to complete each question with a brief answer. At the end of five minutes, most everyone was finished. Johanna then divided six members of the group into separate male and female pairs, and she joined Karen. *"Discuss your responses with your partner,"* she said, *"and talk about the similarities and differences in your answers."*
>
> Johanna could hear some heated discussions taking place, but she concentrated on conversing with Karen, who was born nearly a decade after her. Karen was raised by a single mother. *"I learned to be self-sufficient and not rely on men for anything,"* she shared. After ten minutes, Johanna asked the group to stop their discussions....

GENDER SCRIPTS

Step 3: Reconvene as a group and discuss

Get back together as a large group and ask the members to report on the similarities and differences in their experiences. Ask them the effect of early influences on their current feelings about their own and the opposite sex, and how these feelings might affect their relationships in the workplace.

> *Johanna had to stop...*
> the group discussion after fifteen minutes. *"I'd like to take more time,"* she said, *"but we'll be discussing more after the next worksheet."* All except one female financial analyst, Pauline, had been encouraged to achieve in the workplace. The men also were raised to emphasize achievement. *"Most of you,"* Johanna commented, *"regardless of gender, have the same work goals."*...

Step 4: Complete Worksheet #2, Part I; then discuss Part II with same partner

Distribute Worksheet #2 and ask group members to complete Part I. It should take no longer than five minutes. Have participants return to their original pairs and ask them to select the decade that was most important to them and discuss specific ways men and women were represented by the occupations and professions listed in Part II of the worksheet. Allow ten to fifteen minutes for this discussion.

> *Johanna directed the group to Worksheet #2...*
> and asked them to complete Part I. Within a few minutes, she asked them to return to their discussion partners. *"Choose one or two of the decades listed and discuss the ways in which men and women were depicted by the institutions listed in Part II,"* she instructed. The pairs set to work immediately. She could hear some dissension, but mostly the pairs were intent on listening to each other....

Step 5: Reconvene as a group and discuss

Ask the group members to report on their discussions. Tell them to consider that people from different cultures, ethnic groups, or countries won't necessarily have similar responses. The decade in which one grows up isn't the only determinant of how one views gender.

Summarize by discussing how we are all affected by the time in history in which we grew up, as well as by personal influences such as family, school, and friends.

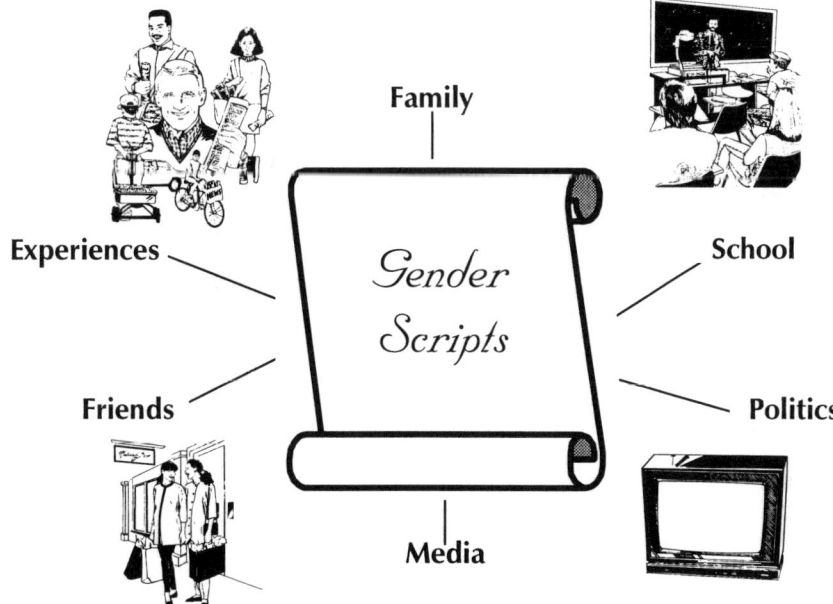

> **"I think it will be easier...**
> *for women born in this decade to compete in the workplace,"* Karen said. *"And a lot harder for the men,"* interjected Alek. *"The rules are continually changing for us."* Johanna encouraged each member to participate, and a healthy discussion followed....

Reinforcing The Lessons Learned

This part is the pivotal point of the whole exercise. If you and your team learn something from *"Gender Scripts"* and use it to the benefit of yourselves and others, then this tool will be a success.

GENDER SCRIPTS

Lessons learned

List the lessons you and your team have learned from using the *"Gender Scripts"* tool.

"Can anyone state...
a lesson we learned from this session?" Johanna asked. *"Other than the fact,"* she quickly added, *"that I grew up in a different decade than most of you."* The department members laughed. *"I've got one,"* Marcelina said. *"I learned that our view of gender is influenced by the environment in which we grew up and by our choice of role models."*

Johanna nodded. *"Anyone else?"* she asked. Curtis jumped in. *"The 'Scripts' from our childhood also influence the way we interpret relationships, the way we process information, and even the way we react to the other gender,"* he said. *"So where do we go from here?"* Johanna asked. *"What can we do with what we've learned?"*

Create an action plan

Work on a plan to use the lessons to your advantage.

Together, the department members...
devised ways in which they could use the lessons learned to improve their work relationships. Their list included:

- ❖ Learn to focus on the content, not the person.
- ❖ Ask yourself: Would I make this request, respond in this way, speak in these terms, etc., if the person I was communicating with was of a different gender?
- ❖ Select another person in the organization and discuss the worksheets with him or her.
- ❖ Come up with three ways to smooth inter-gender relationships and share them at the next meeting.

GENDER SCRIPTS

"Gender Scripts" allow individuals to see how early experiences can influence their attitudes and perceptions about gender. Not all *"scripts"* are bad; this tool lets us identify which we can keep and which we need to erase. And it brings us one step closer to valuing diversity.

TOOLS FOR VALUING DIVERSITY

= GENDER SCRIPTS

GENDER SCRIPTS WORKSHEET #1

Jot down your answers to the following questions. Then, with a partner, discuss the similarities and differences in your answers and explore early *"Gender Scripts."*

1. Where did your present picture of *"a family"* come from? Briefly describe your early family situation, such as the roles of the parents or caregivers or siblings.

2. Which of the last several decades were your most formative years? Who were your role models at that time and how did they influence the way you look at men and women today?

GENDER SCRIPTS

3. Describe some of the messages you received about both men and women *(e.g., "big boys don't cry;" "boys don't hit girls;" "don't worry your pretty little head;" or perhaps, "you should study to be a teacher in case something happens to your husband")*.

_____
_____
_____

4. List some traditional proverbs which may have influenced your "Gender Scripts." *(e.g., "It's a man's world;" "women's work is never done;" "take your medicine like a man;" or "a woman's place is in the home.")*

_____
_____
_____

5. How do you think the messages you received while growing up impact you today when it comes to dealing with someone of the opposite sex?

_____
_____
_____
_____
_____

= GENDER SCRIPTS

GENDER SCRIPTS WORKSHEET #2

Part I

Refer back to the decade you decided was most influential in your early years. Pick a ten-year span and list the ways that both men and women were depicted at that time.

Ten year period from _____ to _____.

Men were depicted as:

_____

_____

Women were depicted as:

_____

_____

Now think about changes which have occurred in more recent times. List the ways that both men and women are depicted now.

Men are currently depicted as:

_____

_____

Women are currently depicted as:

_____

_____

GENDER SCRIPTS

Part II

Describe how men were depicted in various professions during your formative years and how they are depicted today.

	Men Then	Men Now
◆ In Medicine	_____	_____
◆ In Engineering	_____	_____
◆ In Teaching	_____	_____
◆ In the Military	_____	_____
◆ In Politics	_____	_____
◆ In Finance	_____	_____
◆ In Law	_____	_____
◆ In Religion	_____	_____
◆ In Government	_____	_____

GENDER SCRIPTS

Describe how women were depicted in various professions during your formative years and how they are depicted today.

	Women Then	Women Now
◆ In Medicine	_____	_____
◆ In Engineering	_____	_____
◆ In Teaching	_____	_____
◆ In the Military	_____	_____
◆ In Politics	_____	_____
◆ In Finance	_____	_____
◆ In Law	_____	_____
◆ In Religion	_____	_____
◆ In Government	_____	_____

CHAPTER FOUR WORKSHEET: GENDER ISSUES

1. List some of the gender issues that are present in your organization.

2. Would the *"Gender Scripts"* exercise be utilized best as a preventive or as a prescriptive tool in each of the situations described above. Why?

CHAPTER FIVE

DIVERSITY-BASED TEAM BUILDING

Teams and groups are different in nature. While groups are only collections of people, teams are created to accomplish certain objectives. Since members of teams usually work together closely on projects, clear communication and effective skills are critical.

Gaining cooperation among people is necessary for team effectiveness, and dealing with a diverse work team requires special knowledge and sensitivity. People from different cultures, religious backgrounds, ethnic groups, etc., have values and communication styles that may make a significant difference, especially in a team setting. Acknowledging that differences do exist and using those differences to your team's advantage will bring you much closer to accomplishing your team goals.

Why Use *"Diversity-Based Team Building"*

The purpose of *"Diversity-Based Team Building"* is to offer individuals an opportunity to understand the elements of a successful team, as well as to appreciate the impact that diversity has on team effectiveness. Teams rely on their members to help accomplish specific goals. Understanding certain types of approaches to a team effort *(of which many are culturally determined)* is the first step toward utilizing them as strengths.

TOOLS FOR VALUING DIVERSITY

DIVERSITY-BASED TEAM BUILDING

When To Use *"Diversity-Based Team Building"*

Use *"Diversity-Based Team Building"* whenever you want to:

- Increase the effectiveness of interpersonal skills within teams.

- Help teams examine different approaches (many culturally-determined) to a team effort.

- Assist your team members in recognizing that there are cultural dimensions to any diversity-based team effort, and that they can be utilized as strengths.

- Encourage new or already established teams to work together more harmoniously.

Ken Nordstrand, president of a...

small liberal arts college, decided to use *"Diversity-Based Team Building"* at the upcoming faculty retreat that was scheduled right before the fall semester. The faculty, composed of a number of diverse individuals, was complaining that the various committees weren't operating as effectively as they could. Too much dissension and too much wasted time were the top complaints. Since a number of new faculty members were coming on board, Ken felt the team-building tool would prove helpful....

How To Use *"Diversity-Based Team Building"*

To use *"Diversity-Based Team Building,"* complete the following six steps:

Step 1: Start the *"Diversity-Based Team Building"* session

Step 2: Brainstorm definitions of *"team"* and *"group"*

Step 3: List advantages of a team

Step 4: Set up and complete role play

Step 5: Discuss role play in small groups

Step 6: Reconvene as a large group and discuss

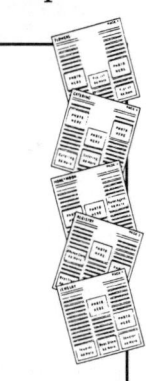

DIVERSITY-BASED TEAM BUILDING

Step 1: Start the *"Diversity-Based Team Building"* session

Set a time limit for the session. Sixty to ninety minutes is usually sufficient. Describe the agenda for the session to your group and agree in advance that all participants will decide on a plan to reinforce the lessons learned by the end of the session.

Make sure your preparations are in order. For *"Diversity-Based Team Building,"* you will need:

- A flip chart and paper
- Paper and markers for participants
- An instruction sheet for each participant (included in this chapter)
- A summary discussion guide for each participant (included in this chapter)
- Enough copies of the role play assignments (in the Appendix), pre-cut into strips

Ken prepared the group...
of forty-one faculty members for the session. With most of the faculty members having had the summer off, they were ready to get down to business. They listened carefully as Ken described the agenda and agreed to come up with an action plan....

Step 2: Brainstorm definitions of *"team"* and *"group"*

Ask the participants to call out words to describe a *"team."* List them on the flip chart and then ask for words that describe a *"group."* List them and discuss how a team differs from a group. Give participants a chance to offer definitions of each and discuss ways to distinguish one from the other. Write their answers on the flip chart.

DIVERSITY-BASED TEAM BUILDING

You may wish to conclude with the following definitions:

> ♦ Group: *A unit formed by a body of people gathered together.*
> ♦ Team: *A unit created to accomplish certain objectives in an efficient way and utilize available resources in a methodical manner.*

Ken asked the faculty members...
to first describe a *"team." "Give me any words that come to your mind,"* he said. They responded quickly, and Ken wrote their responses on the flip chart. Then he asked them to do the same with *"group."* After he finished writing their responses, Ken asked them to define the two terms. They came up with:

Team: A group of individuals set on achieving a specific common goal.
Group: Any number of individuals with at least one common denominator—location, belief, etc....

Step 3: List advantages of a team

Ask the team members to list the advantages of a team over an individual on a given assignment. Record the responses on another page. Ask them to keep these advantages in mind while they do the role play.

Ken flipped to a new page...
on the flip chart. *"Now I'd like you to think of some advantages a team has in completing an assignment,"* he began. *"In contrast, that is, to an individual trying to complete the same assignment."* It was quiet for only a moment. Then the comments flew.

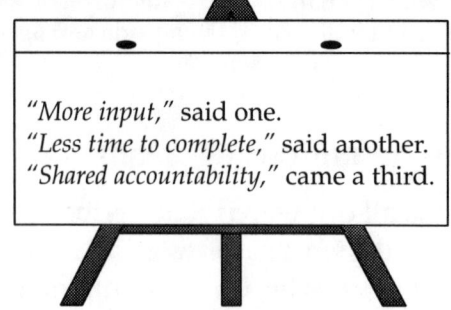

> *"More input,"* said one.
> *"Less time to complete,"* said another.
> *"Shared accountability,"* came a third.

"Hold on a minute," Ken said. *"I can only write so fast."* The faculty members waited, then resumed their comments until the page was full....

DIVERSITY-BASED TEAM BUILDING

Step 4: Set up and complete role play

First, break your larger group into groups of five to seven. Ask group members to take a moment to read the instructions on page 45.

Next, on a random basis, hand out as many different role assignments, copied from the Appendix, as there are people in a group, beginning with assignment A. Each group of seven will use all assignments—A-G. Make sure that no member of a group knows the role assignment of any other member.

Finally, distribute large sheets of paper and markers to each group and ask the group members to complete the assignment within ten minutes. Time them.

> ### *Ken split the forty-one faculty members ...*
> into five groups of seven and one group of six. Then he asked group members to read the instruction sheet. *"Read these first,"* he said. While they were busy reading, Ken took the pre-cut role-assignment strips and passed them out. He did the same with the paper and markers. *"You have ten minutes to complete the role play,"* he instructed, looking at his watch. *"Begin now."* ...

Step 5: Discuss role play in small groups

After time is called, have the group members turn to page 46. If each group has an observer *(role assignment G)*, have him or her lead the group in a discussion as to what went on. If there is no observer *(applies to groups of less than seven members)*, have that group name a discussion leader at the completion of the exercise, and ask him or her to lead the discussion.

DIVERSITY-BASED TEAM BUILDING

Ken stopped the groups...
after ten minutes. Then he asked the group to turn to the summary discussion guides. *"The observer in each group will lead the small group discussion,"* he said, then walked over to the group of six. *"You'll have to choose a discussion leader to lead your discussion,"* he told them. The small groups began to discuss their responses to the role play....

Step 6: Reconvene as a large group and discuss

Allow about ten minutes for this discussion. Have the observer or discussion leader in each group report out loud to the full group. Then ask questions such as:

- Would your group have proceeded differently with a leader?
- What skills could have helped the group progress more effectively?
- What could be done to plan ahead for the next meeting to have things run more smoothly?
- How could you see to it that individual needs were met and that all contributions were respected and accepted?

Ken asked the observers...
in each group to share what had happened in their small group sessions. *"It was a reincarnation of a committee meeting,"* one observer shouted. *"Too many views, too little time."* The faculty members laughed. The discussion brought out some valid points. All agreed that an effective leader or facilitator would be extremely beneficial in any team endeavor. Ken stopped the discussion after ten minutes....

DIVERSITY-BASED TEAM BUILDING

Reinforcing The Lessons Learned

What is the end result of this activity? Can you come up with some concrete lessons you have learned? *"Diversity-Based Team Building"* is designed to help individuals realize the importance of sensitivity and good interpersonal skills in the context of teamwork. Did it do this for your team or group?

Lessons learned

List the lessons you've learned. Even if only a few surface, the exercise will prove valuable.

Ken asked the faculty members...
to come up with a list of lessons they had learned from the role play. They came up with the following:

> **LESSONS LEARNED**
>
> 1. A diverse team needs a leader or facilitator who understands different values and cultures, and is sensitive to the needs of individuals.
>
> 2. A successful team utilizes the strengths of individual members.
>
> 3. Spell out tasks in advance and agree on procedure.

Create an action plan

Once you've devised your list of lessons you have learned from *"Diversity-Based Team Building,"* work with your team or group to create a plan that will help reinforce those lessons.

DIVERSITY-BASED TEAM BUILDING

Ken glanced at his watch...

and said, *"We don't have much time, but this is also the most important segment of the session. We've learned from it. Now we need to transform those lessons into applications for use. Give it some thought. What can we do to apply these lessons?"*

"Each committee should choose as its head a facilitator who is sensitive to cultural approaches," Marcus, a psychology professor, offered. *"If that's not possible,"* he added, *"the committee head should choose a helper who can coach him or her on such issues."*

Ken nodded. *"Good idea,"* he said. *"Any others?"*

"What about clearly defining all tasks," Rolanda, an assistant professor of music, began, *"and also setting clear and definite time limits for completing those tasks. It'll take a lot of guesswork out of the process."*

"Is it possible that each committee could evaluate its effectiveness in these areas?" Ken asked. *"What about filling out an informal survey halfway through each semester? I'll even create the survey."*

"Diversity-Based Team Building" is a tool created to help teams rethink the way they operate. Effective teamwork means viewing each individual team member as an ally; a successful team focuses on how individual differences can increase its capabilities.

DIVERSITY-BASED TEAM BUILDING INSTRUCTION SHEET

You are part of a group of diverse faculty members at a small liberal arts college and have been called together for a high priority, rush job. The college has been chosen for a cover story in a popular magazine. The article has already been written and the group is being asked to design an appropriate cover for the magazine. The design must be at the magazine in another city by 8:00 A.M. tomorrow.

Waiting for you at the magazine's office are artists, photographers, and retouchers. However, your plan must be so clear that they will be able to proceed immediately without any phone calls or questions.

Your task is to create a rough layout, including:

- ♦ The mix of photographs and graphics
- ♦ The balance between people and facilities
- ♦ Specific instructions on who should be included in the pictures
- ♦ Locations where each photo should appear on the cover
- ♦ Whatever copy you think appropriate

Remember, your description *(either in words or diagrams)* has to be perfectly clear and easy to understand. You will be provided with:

- Large Sheet of Paper   • Markers   • Ruler

You each have a role to play and to adhere to at all times. There is no assigned leader. You have ten minutes to accomplish the assignment.

If you finish the task before the allotted time, use the remaining time to design a special team insignia.

DIVERSITY-BASED TEAM BUILDING DISCUSSION GUIDE

Following the Observer Role Assignment, the observer will lead the group discussion, going over the various roles and the feelings of the participants.

The discussion should address these two areas:

1. What actually happened?

2. Identification of problem areas.

Accordingly, the observer will then raise this question, *"Knowing now what you didn't know before, if you were the facilitator or leader, how could you have prepared the participants to overcome any problems that might arise?"*

Chapter Five Worksheet: Building A Diversity-Based Team

1. Use *"Diversity-Based Team Building"* with a team or group in your organization. What key lessons did you learn?

2. What does your action plan entail?

CHAPTER SIX

NONVERBAL EXCHANGES

Communication is a two-way street. It takes both a sender and a receiver, and is the joint responsibility of both parties. Communication is probably one of the most important work skills a person needs. Why? Because communication is necessary in order to get things done.

Yet communication is difficult to get right, because it involves two components—verbal and nonverbal. Research indicates that nonverbal communication is more powerful in giving messages and communicating feelings than verbal communication. But it's also more ambiguous and difficult to interpret accurately. And in today's diverse workplace, when cultural factors enter the picture, communication becomes even more of a challenge.

Why Use *"Nonverbal Exchanges"*

The purpose of this activity is to understand more about communication, particularly nonverbal exchanges. This tool will also help members of your group or team gain insight into the messages that senders may be giving. It will also help them become aware of how these nonverbal messages may be received and interpreted differently, sometimes due to cultural differences.

When To Use *"Nonverbal Exchanges"*

"Nonverbal Exchanges" can be used whenever you want to:

- ♦ Help both individuals and team members increase effective interpersonal communication skills.
- ♦ Make your team members more aware of cultural differences in interpreting nonverbal messages.
- ♦ Build trust and confidence among team members.

TOOLS FOR VALUING DIVERSITY

NONVERBAL EXCHANGES

Leonard, the manager of sales personnel...
at a furniture store in a large metropolitan area, decided to use *"Nonverbal Exchanges"* at his next departmental staff meeting. He was always looking for new ways to increase the effectiveness of his sales team, and he had noticed that they weren't always aware of some of the nonverbal messages they were receiving and sending. Besides, the furniture store catered to a wide variety of clientele, from many different cultures and ethnic backgrounds. *"'Nonverbal Exchanges' may be exactly what we need,"* he thought....

TWO-WAY COMMUNICATION MODEL

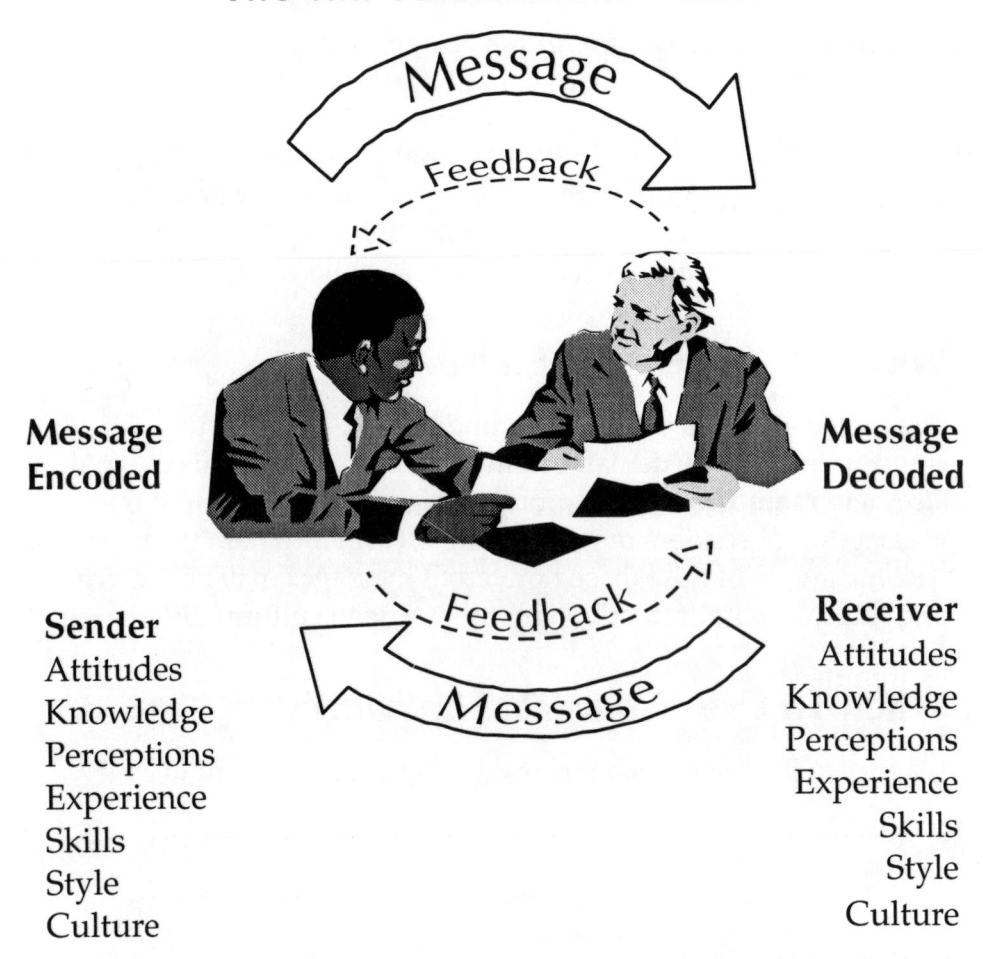

Message → Feedback

Message Encoded

Message Decoded

Feedback ← Message

Sender	**Receiver**
Attitudes	Attitudes
Knowledge	Knowledge
Perceptions	Perceptions
Experience	Experience
Skills	Skills
Style	Style
Culture	Culture

Research shows that over 90% of the information in a two-way communication process is coded and transferred in non-verbal means, making it crucial that both senders and receivers pay attention to what is said and what is conveyed through non-verbal signals.

NONVERBAL EXCHANGES

How To Use *"Nonverbal Exchanges"*

"Nonverbal Exchanges" can be used with just one other person, or with a much larger group. To use this tool effectively, complete the following four steps:

> **Step 1:** Start the *"Nonverbal Exchanges"* session
>
> **Step 2:** Demonstrate the effect of nonverbal messages
>
> **Step 3:** Group participants into pairs and have them complete a *"Nonverbal Exhchanges"* exercise
>
> **Step 4:** Reconvene as a large group and discuss

Step 1: Start the *"Nonverbal Exchanges"* session

Set the *"Nonverbal Exchanges"* session in motion by doing the following:

- Provide a time limit for the session. Generally, forty-five to sixty minutes is sufficient.
- Describe the agenda to your team members.
- Ask that they agree on a plan of action at the end of the session.
- Present a brief description of nonverbal communication, using the introduction to this chapter as your guide. Explain that this session will deal only with nonverbal communication. Also discuss with team members the *"Body Language"* section on pages 57-58.

You will also need a flip chart and marker. In addition, cut copies of the *"Nonverbal Exchanges"* exercise *(in Appendix)* into strips before the session, making sure you have one for each participant.

NONVERBAL EXCHANGES

Leonard called his sales staff...

into the back room and began the session. *"We'll be finished in an hour,"* he said. He laid out the plan for the session and asked all ten members *(Winnie, Brenda, Robert, Carolyn, Luis, Jamal, Mandy, Jake, Gregorio, and Randy)* to commit to coming up with an action plan. They agreed. Leonard asked the group to turn to the *"Two-Way Communication Model"* and explained it to the group. *"I guess it makes sense,"* Jamal commented, *"but I didn't realize that nonverbal messages were such a large part of communication."* Some of the others nodded....

Step 2: Demonstrate the effect of nonverbal messages

Illustrate nonverbal communication by using the following demonstration, which should take about five minutes. Ask a volunteer to stand. Without speaking, use the gesture of a curled finger pointing inward *(typically used to call students to the front of a classroom)*. Let the volunteer come toward you until you want her to stop. Still not speaking, use a raised hand, palm outward as the nonverbal signal for *"stop."*

Thank the volunteer and have her sit down. Discuss with your group the two common nonverbal gestures that you demonstrated. Obviously, most mainstream Americans interpret these to mean *"come here"* and *"stop."* Point out that these gestures also can be used in different ways, depending on a person's cultural background. For example, in some cultures the curled finger is only used for calling animals and prostitutes. The raised palm gesture may also have different meaning and could indicate greetings, innocence, or peace.

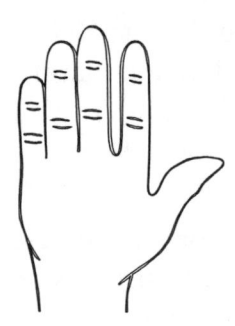

NONVERBAL EXCHANGES

Leonard asked for a volunteer...
and Winnie raised her hand. Leonard proceeded with the demonstration, gesturing for Winnie to come forward. She did until he gestured for her to stop. *"Thanks for your help,"* he said. *"Is that it?"* Winnie asked. *"That was easy."* Leonard smiled. *"It might not have been so easy if you were from a culture who interpreted my first gesture as a call for animals or prostitutes,"* he said. *"Your reaction would have been quite different."* He then continued with an explanation of different interpretations for nonverbal messages....

Step 3: Group participants into pairs and have them complete a "Nonverbal Exchanges" exercise

Divide participants into pairs of individuals who do not know each other well. Using the pre-cut strips of *"Nonverbal Exchanges"* exercise found on page 111 in the Appendix, give one person in each pair a *"sender"* strip and the other, the matching *"receiver"* strip. Sender *"A"* should be paired with Receiver *"A,"* Sender *"B"* with Receiver *"B,"* etc. Make sure that senders and receivers do not share instructions.

Ask group members to read and then follow the instructions provided on their individual pieces of paper. Allow two to three minutes.

Leonard divided the group...
into pairs. He tried to pair staff from the day shift with those who worked primarily evenings so they were less familiar with each other. Then he handed out the slips of paper to each. *"Read only your slip of paper,"* he instructed. *"Do not read that of your partner's."* Leonard gave them a minute to read the instructions. *"Okay, go ahead and start,"* he said.

Leonard walked around the room, observing the pairs. Brenda and Carolyn were given the pair *"B"* exchange. As the sender, Brenda was instructed to move closer and closer to Carolyn, while finding out two new things about her. Carolyn was given the direction to stand up and answer questions. As Brenda got closer, Leonard observed discomfort on Carolyn's part. She folded her arms and leaned backwards. After a few minutes, Leonard asked the pairs to stop....

TOOLS FOR VALUING DIVERSITY

NONVERBAL EXCHANGES

Step 4: Reconvene as a large group and discuss

Ask the pairs to return to the group and ask the A, B, and C receivers, and the D senders, to describe what nonverbal communication messages they received in this exercise. Record their responses on the flip chart. Ask them which was more significant—what was said verbally or what was said nonverbally.

Explain that you handed out four different sets of instructions:

- The nonverbal message in group *"A"* demonstrated eye contact and the use of body language.
- The nonverbal message in group *"B"* demonstrated the use of space.
- The nonverbal message in group *"C"* demonstrated tone.
- The nonverbal message in group *"D"* demonstrated mixed messages.

Discuss the *"Body Language"* section *(pages 57-58)* with each group member. Point out that interpretation of nonverbal messages may vary depending on the cultural background of the individual, and explain that when communicating with the diverse work force, it is important to be able to recognize and correctly interpret nonverbal cues.

NONVERBAL EXCHANGES

When the group reconvened...
Leonard stepped up to the flip chart. *"Those of you who were receivers in the A, B, and C exchanges, and whoever was the sender in the D exchange, think about what was said and what wasn't said,"* he began. *"What nonverbal messages did you receive?"*

Luis spoke up. *"I was an 'A' receiver,"* he said. *"And Robert, my partner, asked me what my favorite movie was, and why. While I was telling him, he crossed his arms and his legs and wouldn't even look at me. Then he said I made a great choice and he agreed with me. But he didn't even look at me while he was talking. I felt like he was blowing me off."*

The others made similar comments, and all agreed that the nonverbal messages had more impact in these situations. Leonard asked the group to turn to the *"Body Language"* section, and the staff discussed the different types of messages nonverbal communication conveys, American use of space, and how other cultures may interpret body language differently. After twenty minutes, Leonard stopped the discussion....

Reinforcing The Lessons Learned

This is the crucial part of the whole exercise. Check to see if you and your team learned something from *"Nonverbal Exchanges"* and can use what you learned to improve.

Lessons learned

List the lessons you and your team have learned from using the *"Nonverbal Exchanges"* tool.

"We're nearing the end...
of the session," Leonard said. *"Remember what we agreed upon at the beginning? We need to figure out what we've learned from this exercise in nonverbal communication. Help me out here. What did you learn?"* The sales staff wasn't silent for long. They came up with the following lessons....

NONVERBAL EXCHANGES

LESSONS LEARNED

- Nonverbal messages are a large part of communication.
- Nonverbal messages are more difficult to read, especially if cultural differences exist.
- We need to be more aware of and sensitive to nonverbal messages if we desire to improve communication.

Create an action plan

Now devise a plan to use the lessons you have learned.

"You've learned some...
good lessons," Leonard said. "But the real test of this exercise is whether you can put them to use. Unless you can, you haven't really learned anything. Does anyone have an idea of how we can act on what we've learned?"

Jamal spoke up. "What if we consciously use nonverbal messages with others and check their responses? We might learn more or at least we'll remember what we've already learned." Carolyn nodded and added, "I think we should meet again to talk more about how we can use or interpret nonverbal messages." Leonard seconded that notion and agreed that they could discuss the same topic at the next staff meeting.

Brenda raised her hand. "I'd like to know more about different cultural interpretations of body language. Maybe we could split into groups and take a different culture to research. Then we could report our findings at the next meeting. I think it would help increase our sales." The staff thought it was a good idea, and Leonard created a sign-up sheet so members could choose a culture to research.

"Nonverbal Exchanges" provide insight into the nonverbal messages we send and receive whenever communication takes place. And since communication is far from being an exact science, we must be more aware of the effect of nonverbal messages, especially in a diverse workplace. When we learn to communicate effectively with all different individuals, then we're on the right path toward valuing diversity.

NONVERBAL EXCHANGES

BODY LANGUAGE

In addition to the spoken word, people communicate using their bodies. Elements of nonverbal communication are important in communicating across cultures.

Nonverbal Communication such as:

- Facial expressions: smiles, frowns, nods
- Gestures: pointing, beckoning, shrugging
- Body position: arms crossed, legs crossed, head tilted
- Posture: leaning forward, leaning backward
- Contact: eye contact, handshaking, kissing, touching, back slapping

Gives rise to messages, such as:

- Affection
- Appreciation
- Boredom
- Embarrassment
- Impatience
- Warning
- Anger
- Power

You may not be sending the message you intended when dealing with people of diverse backgrounds.

You may be misinterpreting the sender's message and making assumptions about the meaning of their nonverbal communication.

TOOLS FOR VALUING DIVERSITY • REPRODUCIBLE FORM

NONVERBAL EXCHANGES

BODY LANGUAGE

"Mainstream" American use of space

People are curious about differences in the use of space in conversation. Researchers have identified four categories:

> **Intimate:** From actual contact to about 18 inches. Generally used by family and close friends.
>
> **Personal:** From 18 inches to about 4 feet. Normal conversation, friends and acquaintances.
>
> **Social:** From 4 feet to about 7 feet—impersonal conversation and business transactions. From 7 feet to about 12 feet—seating arrangements in formal social or business relationships.
>
> **Public:** From 12 feet or more. Training, teaching, and presentations in front of large groups.

Other cultures may be very different

In other cultures, closer distances or contact is more prevalent:

- Casual male friends hold hands
- Males greet each other with kisses instead of handshakes
- Males are likely to put their arms around one another
- Businessmen stand much closer

In some cultures, power and hierachal respect are shown by greater distances:

- Bowing is used as a greeting
- High-ranking business and political figures are not to be approached too closely, granting them distance according to their status.

Chapter Six Worksheet: Communicating Beyond Words

1. Describe the communication styles and nuances *(both verbal and nonverbal)* within your team or group.

2. How do you think *"Nonverbal Exchanges"* would benefit your team?

3. Complete the *"Nonverbal Exchanges"* exercise with your team. What lessons did you learn?

CHAPTER SEVEN

COMMUNICATING INTERCULTURALLY

Because people are unique, they differ in their values, perceptions, and how they communicate and solve problems. The communication process is further complicated by cultural differences. Resolving communication problems is critical to success in a diverse workplace.

Why Use *"Communicating Interculturally"*

The purpose of *"Communicating Interculturally"* is to offer an opportunity to discuss culture clashes and to analyze several situations in light of good intercultural communication practices. *"Communicating Interculturally"* provides the Feedback Planner to help resolve communication problems across cultures. The Feedback Planner may be used as a guide to develop skills for dealing with people from other cultures.

When To Use *"Communicating Interculturally"*

Use *"Communicating Interculturally"* whenever you:

- ♦ notice that cultural clashes are impacting your team or group.

- ♦ want to provide your team members with a practical approach for resolving communication problems.

- ♦ seek to improve communication skills in your diverse team or work group.

COMMUNICATING INTERCULTURALLY

> ***Karina, manager of a manufacturing plant team ...***
> was unhappy with the way her team was behaving. *"They're constantly talking about one another,"* she confided to a colleague, *"and they never seem to get along."* Her colleague suggested she use *"Communicating Interculturally."* *"It's a tool designed to promote better communication among different kinds of people,"* he explained. Karina checked it out and decided to use it at the next team meeting....

How To Use *"Communicating Interculturally"*

Using *"Communicating Interculturally"* involves the following four steps:

Step 1: Start the *"Communicating Interculturally"* session

Step 2: Break into groups of three or four and assign case studies *(in the Appendix)*

Step 3: Report and discuss the different responses

Step 4: Distribute handout and discuss

Step 1: Start the *"Communicating Interculturally"* session

Set a time limit for the session. Forty-five to sixty minutes is usually sufficient. Describe the agenda for the session to your group and agree in advance that all participants will decide on a plan to reinforce the lessons learned by the end of the session.

Prepare for your session by having enough copies of the case studies and the Feedback Planner handout for each member of your group. You can find these pages in the Appendix. You may also want to use a flip chart for writing the responses you want the small groups to discuss in Step 2.

COMMUNICATING INTERCULTURALLY

Karina started the session...
by asking the seventeen team members to listen carefully. *"In the next hour,"* she said, *"we will be learning how to communicate better with one another."* Some raised their eyebrows, but they did pay attention as Karina described the agenda and asked for their help in coming up with an action plan....

Step 2: Break into groups of three or four and assign case studies

Divide your team or group into smaller groups of three to four individuals. Give each person a copy of the intercultural case studies *(found in the Appendix)* and ask everyone to read them. Allow a few minutes for this. Then assign one case study to each group.

Allow about ten to fifteen minutes for each group to discuss the following:

- What was happening in our case study?
- How did culture play a part?
- How could the situation have been handled?
- Could the conflict have been avoided in the first place?

Karina separated the team members...
into three groups of three members, and two groups of four. *"I'm giving each one of you a copy of the case studies we'll be discussing,"* she began. *"So take a few minutes to read them."*

When she noticed that all were done reading, she assigned a case study to each group. On a flip chart, she had written the questions she wanted each group to discuss, and she asked them to look at the chart and begin their discussions....

Step 3: Report and discuss the different responses

Ask each group to report the responses to their case study. Then discuss the responses as a large group.

> *Karina stopped the small-group...*
> discussions after fifteen minutes. *"It sounds as if you had a lot to discuss,"* she commented. Each of the groups briefly relayed their group discussions, and the team as a whole talked about the responses. *"It appears that you didn't find these situations easy to handle,"* Karina said. *"And they're not that easy. But there is a model of intercultural communication that could be very helpful in these cases, and I'd like to show it to you."* ...

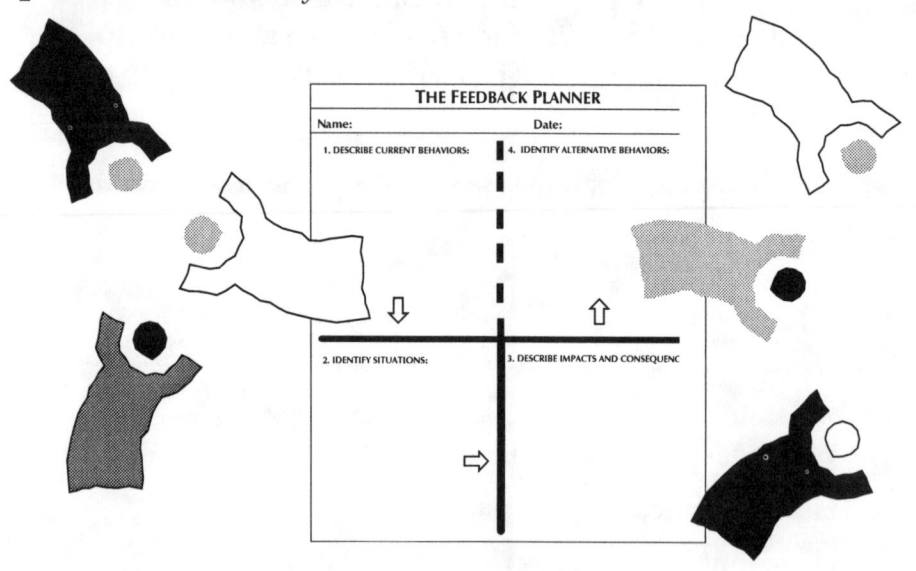

```
              THE FEEDBACK PLANNER
Name:                         Date:
1. DESCRIBE CURRENT BEHAVIORS:  | 4. IDENTIFY ALTERNATIVE BEHAVIORS:
                                |
                                |
            ⇩                   ⇧
2. IDENTIFY SITUATIONS:         | 3. DESCRIBE IMPACTS AND CONSEQUENC[ES]
                                |
            ⇨
```

Step 4: Distribute handout and discuss

Give a copy of the Feedback Planner handout to each participant. Take time to discuss it and summarize by discussing the importance of developing communication skills to manage diversity. Point out how each case study could have been handled in terms of the Feedback Planner. The Feedback Planner is an effective way to provide immediate feedback to reinforce *(through praise)* or redirect *(through criticism)* behavior to improve a situation. Also, the Feedback Planner is a note-taking worksheet that helps you collect and analyze your thoughts about a situation prior to discussing it with another person. If time permits, each group should role play its case study using the Feedback Planner.

COMMUNICATING INTERCULTURALLY

THE FEEDBACK PLANNER	
Name:	**Date:**
1. DESCRIBE CURRENT BEHAVIORS: Describe current behaviors that you want to reinforce (praise) or redirect (criticism) to improve a situation. *There have been mock racist comments and jokes made in the group about the new lead operator.* ⬇	**4. IDENTIFY ALTERNATIVE BEHAVIORS:** Identify alternative behaviors and actions for you, the employee, and others to take. *We can talk to those involved privately, explain to them how they are hurting someone, and ask them to treat everyone with the same respect they would like to receive if they were the other person.* ⬆
2. IDENTIFY SITUATIONS: Identify the specific times, places and circumstances when the comments were heard or the behaviors were observed. *In the most recent situation, just this week, a routine work request was met with the response, "Yassir, Boss."* ➡	**3. DESCRIBE IMPACTS AND CONSEQUENCES:** Describe impacts and consequences of the current behaviors. *This type of behavior, even when delivered as a joke, is difficult to take that way, and causes resentment, disrupting the work environment.*

Karina distributed...

the handouts and asked each member to take a close look. "*Using the Feedback Planner is a practical approach to dealing with communication problems,*" she said. They discussed the model for a few minutes; then Karina asked them how they would use it in the case studies. One employee, Maria, spoke up. "*My group had the first case study,*" she said. "*It's the one where a racist comment is made jokingly, and a person's hurt by it. I think I'd talk to the individual who told the joke, but I wouldn't do it in front of the hurt person. That might embarrass him.*" Karina nodded and listened as Maria continued. The rest of the group joined the discussion; before long, they had discussed all the case studies....

COMMUNICATING INTERCULTURALLY

Reinforcing The Lessons Learned

Your group discussions should lead you to uncover some lessons learned from this activity and help you create an action plan to communicate differently as a result. *"Communicating Interculturally"* is a practical tool that's meant to be used. Work together with your team or group to put it in action.

Lessons learned

What are the lessons you have learned in this session? List them.

> ### *Karina was pleased...*
> with the discussions. *"You've done a great job applying the Feedback Planner to the case studies,"* she said. *"But here comes the clincher. I need you to tell me what lessons you've learned from this activity."* Karina started writing on the flip chart as the team came up with a list....

LESSONS LEARNED

1. Communication problems are very common in the workplace.

2. A diverse workplace often has more communication problems.

3. We need to be sensitive to differences in communication.

4. We need to develop skills for dealing with people of different cultures, ethnic background, gender, etc.

Create an action plan

Once you've come up with a list of lessons you have learned from "Communicating Interculturally," ask your team or group to create a plan that will help reinforce those lessons.

Karina turned over...

the sheet on the flip chart. *"Good job,"* she said. *"Now we're ready to take those lessons and determine how we can make them work for us. Any ideas?"* The team members thought, then started responding. Together, they came up with the following ideas:

Action Plan

- Practice using the Feedback Planner at home or outside the workplace, in order to master the skills.

- Use the Feedback Planner in a current work situation.

- Report back to the group about the experiences and discuss.

"Communicating Interculturally" can make a great difference in the way your team or group relates to others in the workplace. The key is learning how to use the Feedback Planner, and then actually using it. If you can encourage your team members to do that, you'll have overcome a major obstacle in capitalizing on workplace diversity.

CHAPTER SEVEN WORKSHEET: BRIDGING INTERCULTURAL COMMUNICATION GAPS

1. List two recent work situations where the Feedback Planner would have helped.

   _____
   _____
   _____
   _____
   _____

2. Choose one of the two situations listed in number one, and describe how you would have used the Feedback Planner in that situation.

   _____
   _____
   _____
   _____
   _____
   _____
   _____

COMMUNICATING INTERCULTURALLY

3. Use *"Communicating Interculturally"* with a group or team in your organization. What action plan did you create?

CHAPTER EIGHT

LISTENING COMPETENCY

Listening is one of the most important communication skills. Without careful listening, messages often are misinterpreted and people do not feel valued or understood. Too often people take listening for granted and do not pay enough attention to the speaker. In the case of communicating in diverse work groups, the act of listening becomes even more critical because there are additional factors such as accents, idioms, and slang.

Why Use *"Listening Competency"*

The purpose of *"Listening Competency"* is to ensure that participants are aware of the importance of listening, and have an opportunity to assess their present listening skills. Tips are also provided on listening to those who speak limited English.

When To Use *"Listening Competency"*

Use the *"Listening Competency"* tool whenever you want to:

- Reinforce the importance of careful listening, especially when dealing with people of different cultures and/or who speak limited English.

- Help your team members pay closer attention to others.

- Improve communication skills and build interpersonal relationships within your team or group.

LISTENING COMPETENCY

Carl, a restaurant manager...
recently noticed that communication problems were resulting from his servers not listening. Problems especially surfaced when the servers conversed with those who spoke little English, whether they were customers or kitchen help. Carl decided to use *"Listening Competency"* at the upcoming servers' meeting....

How To Use *"Listening Competency"*

"Listening Competency" can be used individually, in teams, or with others of your choice. If you use this tool with others, complete the following five steps:

Step 1: Start the *"Listening Competency"* session

Step 2: Discuss good listening skills

Step 3: Group into pairs for discussion

Step 4: Complete *"Listening Competency: A Self Assessment"* and discuss

Step 5: Review *"Tips For Improved Listening With Those Speaking Limited English"* and discuss

---

Step 1: Start the *"Listening Competency"* session

Set a time limit for your *"Listening Competency"* session. Thirty to forty minutes generally is sufficient for this exercise. Describe to the members of your group what will take place during the session and gain acceptance for creating a plan to reinforce the lessons learned.

Make sure you have a flip chart and marker. Also have available enough copies of the *"Listening Competency: A Self Assessment"* for the members of your group. *(These may be found in the Appendix.)* Provide a pencil or pen for each individual.

Carl counted heads...

and noted that all fifteen of his servers were present. *"It's time to listen,"* he began, *"especially since our meeting today revolves around listening."* The group quieted down. Carl explained what was taking place and asked for their assistance. They all agreed....

Step 2: Discuss good listening skills

Talk to your group about the importance of good listening. Ask the group members, *"In your jobs, why is it important to be a good listener?"* Record the answers on the flip chart. Then ask them, *"Does it make a difference when you are communicating with someone from another race or culture, or someone who speaks a different native language?"* If the answer is yes, discuss how, and add their comments to the flip chart.

Carl walked up to the flip chart...

and took the top off the marker. *"Is good listening important?"* he asked the servers. *"You bet,"* answered Jerry, one of the night servers. *"If I don't listen to my girlfriend, she'll pout."* Some of the others snickered. *"Okay,"* responded Carl. *"You've established one reason for good listening. But what about at work? Why is it important to be a good listener on the job?"*

Linda, one of the day servers, spoke up. *"If we don't listen to the customers, we might get the order wrong. And that would be a disaster!"* she commented. *"Good response,"* Carl said. *"Anyone else?"* The group came up with various comments, which Carl wrote on the flip chart. Then Carl asked whether communicating with someone from a different culture should make a difference to a listener. The servers thought and decided that listening would be even more important....

> "Does it make a difference when you are communicating with someone from another race or culture, or someone who speaks a different native language?"

LISTENING COMPETENCY

Step 3: Group into pairs for discussion

Divide your group into pairs and ask them to describe a situation where miscommunication occurred due to lack of listening. Give them an example, such as a listener thinking ahead about a response and not giving full attention to the speaker. The listener might unknowingly agree to something the speaker asks him to do, which could cause problems if he never follows through.

> *Carl asked the servers...*
> to find a partner, and he joined Tran, a recently hired, part-time server. "Can you think of a situation?" Carl asked. "Yes," Tran responded. "Just the other day, one of the bus boys asked me if I wanted a table cleared," he said. "I have trouble understanding him, and I suppose I don't listen carefully enough, but I thought he asked me if I needed another set of silverware. So I told him, 'Yes,' and he cleared the table while the diner and her daughter were in the bathroom." Tran laughed. "It's funny now, but it wasn't then. I hadn't even served their dinner yet, and he cleared their half-eaten salads, drinks, everything."...

Step 4: Complete *"Listening Competency: A Self Assessment"* and discuss

Distribute a self-assessment to those attending the session and ask each person to answer the questions. Then, using the instructions provided, all group members should score their assessments.

After the assessments are completed and scored, ask for a show of hands of those who are considered good listeners based on their scores. How many are surprised by their scores? Stress that even good listeners require constant practice in concentrating. Tell the group that they now know what to work on in order to become better listeners.

LISTENING COMPETENCY

> *Carl handed out...*
> the listening self-inventories and pencils. *"Read each question carefully,"* he instructed. *"Then check one of the five answers. When you are finished, follow the directions for scoring. Be honest. I'm not going to grade you on this. It's for your benefit."* When the servers finished, Carl asked them for their results. Many thought they were better listeners than the inventory showed....

Step 5: Review *"Tips For Improved Listening With Those Speaking Limited English"* and discuss

Have each member of your team or group review *"Tips For Improved Listening With Those Speaking Limited English."* Explain that listening can be difficult when communicating with anyone; however, it is much more complicated when cultural factors come into play. Review the tips below and ask for any additional suggestions.

TIPS FOR IMPROVED LISTENING WITH THOSE SPEAKING LIMITED ENGLISH

- Give the speaker your full attention
- Be comfortable with silence and long pauses
- Be patient
- Be aware of nonverbal cues that may signal a lack of understanding
- Recognize that the person may be having difficulty saying exactly what he/she means
- Concentrate on what is being said; this will help overcome the barrier of accent
- Be aware of your own biases and how they may interfere with your ability to listen
- Remember that communication styles differ
- When waiting for a response, pause longer to allow the other person enough time to answer
- Allow those with limited English to finish sentences and thoughts for themselves

LISTENING COMPETENCY

Carl pointed to...
the *"Tips For Improved Listening With Those Speaking Limited English."* "These tips may be a lifesaver for you," Carl explained. "We have many customers from different cultures, and a number of the kitchen staff don't speak much English." Together, they went over the tips and discussed how each could help....

Reinforcing The Lessons Learned

Every exercise in this guidebook has lessons built into it. Your job is to choose the lessons you have learned and decide how they can help you improve.

Lessons learned

List the lessons you and your team have learned from using the *"Listening Competency"* tool.

"Okay," Carl said...
"We're to the point in our meeting where we need to decide what we've learned. What have you learned from this exercise?" For a moment, it was quiet. Then the group came up with ideas that were condensed into the following three lessons learned....

LESSONS LEARNED

1. Good listening is critical in any workplace situation.

2. Good listening skills often need to be developed.

3. Good listening is even more important when dealing with those of other cultures and/or those who speak limited English.

LISTENING COMPETENCY

Create an action plan

Now work on a plan to use the lessons to your advantage.

> *Carl ended the discussion...*
> on lessons learned by asking, *"What can we do with the lessons we've learned? How can we put them to work for us to help us improve our listening skills?"* The servers came up with the following list:

- From the 18 listening competencies on the Self-Assessment, select two or three you would like to improve. What can be done to become a better listener in those areas?

- In conversations (work-related or personal), practice becoming a better listener.

- When conversing with those who speak limited English, follow the tips from this chapter (e.g., pause, give full attention, allow speakers to finish their own thoughts, etc.).

- At your next group meeting, retake the self-inventory and compare current scores with initial scores.

"Listening Competency" allows individuals to understand the importance of good listening and to realize that constant practice is often necessary to improve listening skills. In addition, cultural considerations increase the need for good listening skills. When we learn to communicate and listen effectively to individuals of diverse backgrounds, we break down barriers and build trust.

Chapter Eight Worksheet: Learning To Listen

1. Think about your team or group. Have you noticed any situations where better listening skills would have helped? Describe them.

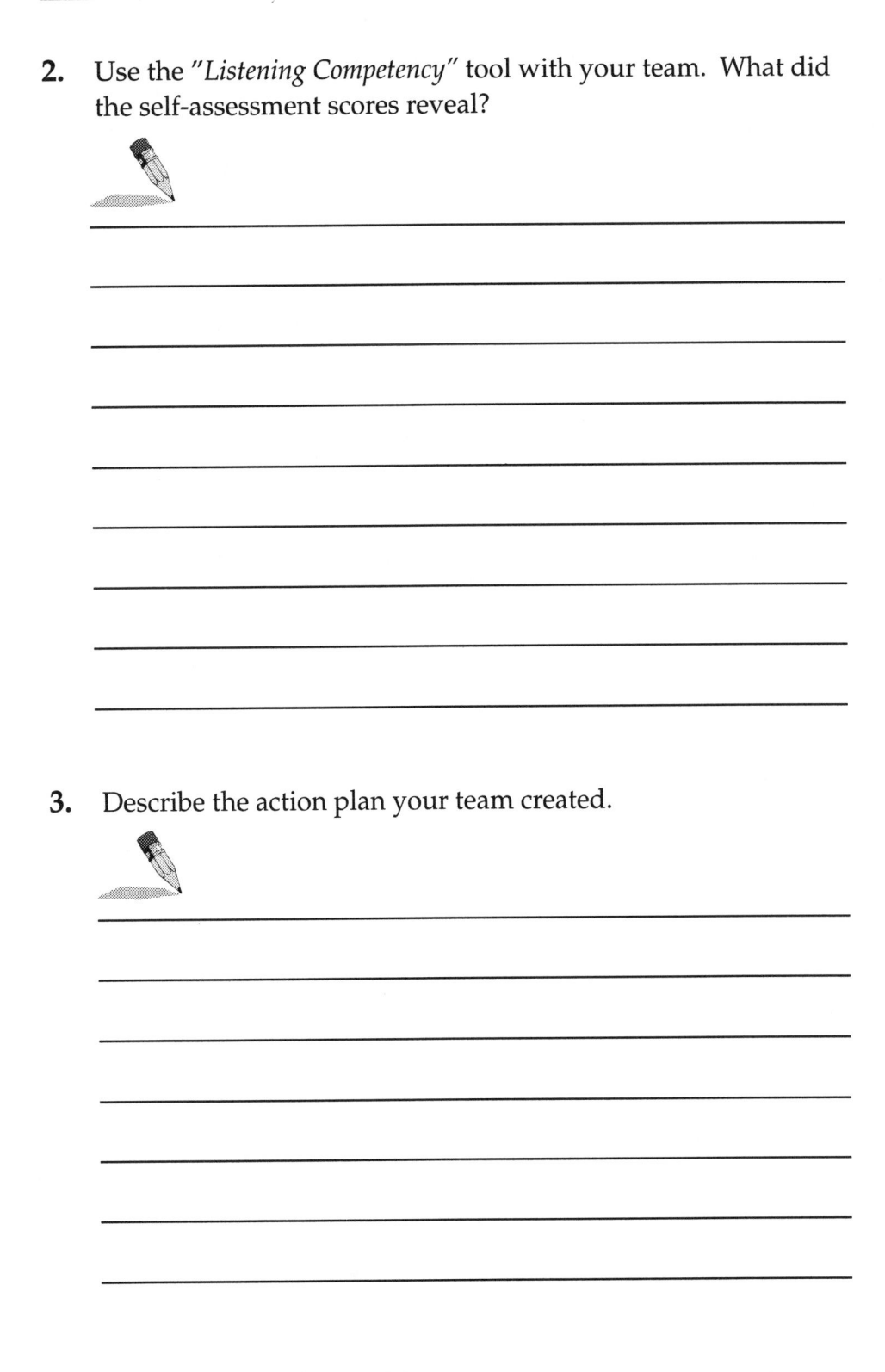

LISTENING COMPETENCY

2. Use the *"Listening Competency"* tool with your team. What did the self-assessment scores reveal?

_____
_____
_____
_____
_____
_____
_____
_____
_____

3. Describe the action plan your team created.

_____
_____
_____
_____
_____
_____
_____

CHAPTER NINE

DIVERSITY-BASED CONFLICT RESOLUTION

Conflict management styles vary from person to person. Differences in values, perceptions, and beliefs all contribute to one's own style of resolving conflict. And cultural differences cannot be overlooked. In some cultures, verbal conflict is avoided at all costs. Other groups encourage arguing, and the more heated the conflict becomes, the better everyone feels.

The way people describe conflict says much about their style. For example, many mainstream American males use sports language when discussing a dispute: *"You threw me a curve," "I was blind-sided,"* or even *"Time out!" (hands forming a "T")*. Compare this approach with others who believe in saving face and achieving harmony. Cultural considerations are important when managing conflict.

PUMPED UP   BLIND-SIDED

Why Use *"Diversity-Based Conflict Resolution"*

"Diversity-Based Conflict Resolution" is a tool designed to help members of your team or group understand that conflict is a natural occurrence in interpersonal relationships and that everyone has different styles in dealing with conflict situations. It will help your team members identify their own particular styles and learn ways to resolve conflict effectively. A workplace that values diversity has employees who know how to resolve diversity-based conflicts.

DIVERSITY CONFLICT RESOLUTION

When To Use *"Diversity-Based Conflict Resolution"*

"Diversity-Based Conflict Resolution" can be used whenever:

- ◆ Your team has more than its share of conflicts.
- ◆ Your team members' styles of managing conflict hinder effective resolution.
- ◆ You want your team members to be more aware of cultural differences in conflict resolution.
- ◆ You want to increase harmony among team members.

Jill, the unit coordinator for Skyline Hospital's...
fifth floor, knew that her nurses needed help in managing conflict. More and more conflicts were erupting over the smallest details, and it wasn't getting better. Jill talked with Patty, the night-shift coordinator, and the two decided to use *"Diversity-Based Conflict Resolution"* at the next staff meeting....

How To Use *"Diversity-Based Conflict Resolution"*

"Diversity-Based Conflict Resolution" can be used by completing the following six steps:

Step 1: Start the *"Diversity-Based Conflict Resolution"* session

Step 2: Group in pairs and discuss work-related conflicts

Step 3: Explain the *"Overview of Conflict"*

Step 4: Set up and complete role play

Step 5: Reconvene in a large group and discuss

Step 6: Discuss *"Conflict Resolution Styles"*

DIVERSITY CONFLICT RESOLUTION

Step 1: Start the *"Diversity-Based Conflict Resolution"* session

Begin the *"Diversity-Based Conflict Resolution"* session by doing the following:

- Provide a time limit for the session. Generally, sixty to ninety minutes is sufficient.
- Describe the agenda to your team members.
- Ask that they agree on a plan of action at the end of the session.

Jill called the staff meeting...
to order and asked Patty to describe the agenda. When Patty finished, Jill asked for cooperation in coming up with an action plan at the end of the session. The fourteen nurses in attendance agreed. *"Thank you,"* Jill responded. *"I'm glad we didn't have a conflict over that."* The nurses laughed....

Step 2: Group in pairs and discuss work-related conflicts

Divide your team into pairs and ask them to talk about work-related conflict situations they have seen or of which they have been a part. Have them discuss:

1. The reasons that conflict occurs,
2. The sources of conflict in general, and
3. Behaviors that contribute to, or result from, the conflict.

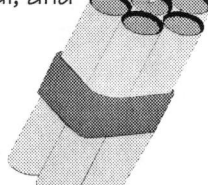

TOOLS FOR VALUING DIVERSITY

Jill asked the nurses...

to find a partner. *"I want you to talk about work conflicts you've witnessed or which you were a part of."* As Jill continued, Patty wrote on the flip chart the three items Jill wanted the pairs to discuss. Then the two coordinators walked around the room, listening to the discussions that were taking place. One nurse, Rishma, was describing to her partner, Agnes, an episode where she and another nurse had disagreed about the schedule. *"Both of us wanted July 4th off, but I gave in,"* Rishma said. Other nurses talked about sharing workloads, not getting the help they needed, and attitudes that needed changing....

Step 3: Explain the "Overview of Conflict"

Have each team member review the *"Overview of Conflict."* Talk briefly about the reasons behind conflict, the sources of conflict, and the behavioral characteristics of conflict.

Review the *"Overview of Conflict"* diagram below and *"Conflict Resolution Styles"* located toward the end of the chapter to ensure team members are making the same distinction between the underlying reasons behind a conflict, sources of a conflict, and the behaviors we exhibit/observe in conflicts. You will also need to cut copies of the *"Role-Play Situations" (in the Appendix)* into strips, making sure you have one slip of paper for each individual. Have group members focus on the *"Observer Guidelines" (on page 90)* for each group of three. In addition, you need to provide a flip chart, marker, and a pencil or pen for each observer.

Overview Of Conflict

Reasons Behind Conflict
- Different perceptions
- Incorrect assumptions
- Dissimilar values

Source of Conflict
- Lack of resources
- Divergent goals

Behavioral Characteristics
- Miscommunication *(sometimes due to language differences)*
- Interrupting
- Blocking ideas
- Not listening
- Controlling the discussion

DIVERSITY CONFLICT RESOLUTION

> ***Patty reviewed the "Overview of Conflict"...***
> while Jill explained it. *"It didn't seem as if anyone was at a loss for words when we were discussing actual conflicts,"* Jill began, *"so I'm sure you'll all agree that conflict is very common."* No one disagreed. Jill continued, discussing the different aspects of conflict and asking for comments from the group....

Step 4: Set up and complete role play

Divide into groups of three. Ask the groups to identify one individual in each group as the *"observer."* Have each observer review the *"Observer Guidelines"* on page 90. Distribute to the two remaining participants in each group a single situation from *"Role-Play Situations."* One will receive a pre-cut *"A"* slip; the other, a "B" slip. Make sure none of the three share instructions.

Observer

Allow five to ten minutes for the paired participants to role play the situation, during which their goal is to resolve the conflict. At the same time, the observer follows his guidelines. Note: Three situation role plays are provided. You may add your own or use the same ones for several groups.

> ***Jill divided the fourteen nurses...***
> into groups of three. Patty joined one group to make it even. *"Each group must choose one person to be the observer,"* Jill instructed. *"That person will receive guidelines to follow. Please don't share your guidelines with the other members of your group."* Jill asked the group to turn to the *"Observer Guidelines,"* then distributed role-play situations to the others in each group. *"Read only your situation,"* she said. *"Then begin the role play. Your goal is to resolve the conflict."*...

Step 5: Reconvene in a large group and discuss

When the groups are finished with their role plays, ask them to rejoin the large group. Then ask the observers to read their situations and report on what happened in the role play.

DIVERSITY CONFLICT RESOLUTION

When everyone was done...

with their role plays, Jill called them together. *"Now the observers can tell us what happened. Read the situation,"* she told the observers, *"and tell us how your pair resolved it."* Patty, who was the observer for her group, volunteered to be first. *"Our situation was number two, and the conflict revolved around which department member got to attend a prepaid conference in Hawaii,"* she said. *"Both were equally qualified. Charito gave in to Norma. There wasn't a great deal of competition. Norma said she wanted to go, Charito said she did too, but that she'd let Norma go."* The other observers also shared what took place during their role plays....

Step 6: Discuss "Conflict Resolution Styles"

Have your team members read and discuss *"Conflict Resolution Styles"* found towards the end of this chapter. Ask them to share their identified styles and whether or not they used those styles in the role plays. Also ask if they observed the use of other styles in their role plays.

Have team members state the skills they feel are necessary to resolve conflict and record their responses on the flip chart. Summarize by discussing *"Ways To Resolve Conflict."*

Ways To Resolve Conflict

- Respect each person
- Encourage opponents to openly discuss the situation
- Listen to all sides of the story
- Determine specific issues
- Identify the styles of conflict
- Appreciate differing opinions
- Engage employees in exploring alternatives and positive outcomes
- Look for common ground

DIVERSITY CONFLICT RESOLUTION

After the nurses read...

"Conflict Resolution Styles" and shared what they felt were their styles, Jill pointed out that the most useful style is *"Cooperation." "But,"* Jill included, *"there are times when other styles are more appropriate. What's important is being aware of your own style and recognizing others', so that you can anticipate how they might react. Then you can adjust your style to fit."* She paused for a moment, then added, *"Conflict resolution styles might also differ because of culture. Consider cultural differences when you're having a conflict with someone of another culture."* Next, Patty discussed *"Ways To Resolve Conflict"* and asked the nurses what they thought of the ideas. A lively discussion ensued....

Reinforcing The Lessons Learned

"Diversity-Based Conflict Resolution" is full of information and applicable lessons. See if you and your team can identify some of the lessons and create a plan for using them.

Lessons learned

Have you and your team learned any lessons from *"Diversity-Based Conflict Resolution"*? Now is the time to mention them.

The nurses came up...

with the following lessons they learned:

LESSONS LEARNED

1. Conflict is a normal part of life.

2. Conflict styles vary, sometimes due to cultural backgrounds.

3. Understanding personal and others' styles of conflict can help in the successful resolution of conflicts.

4. Knowing there are ways to resolve conflict, and using them, also helps one successfully resolve conflict.

DIVERSITY CONFLICT RESOLUTION

Create an action plan

What can you do with the lessons you've learned? Work on formulating an action plan.

> ***Once the nurses had identified...***
> the lessons they had learned, it was relatively easy to come up with an action plan. Their action plan consisted of the following ideas:

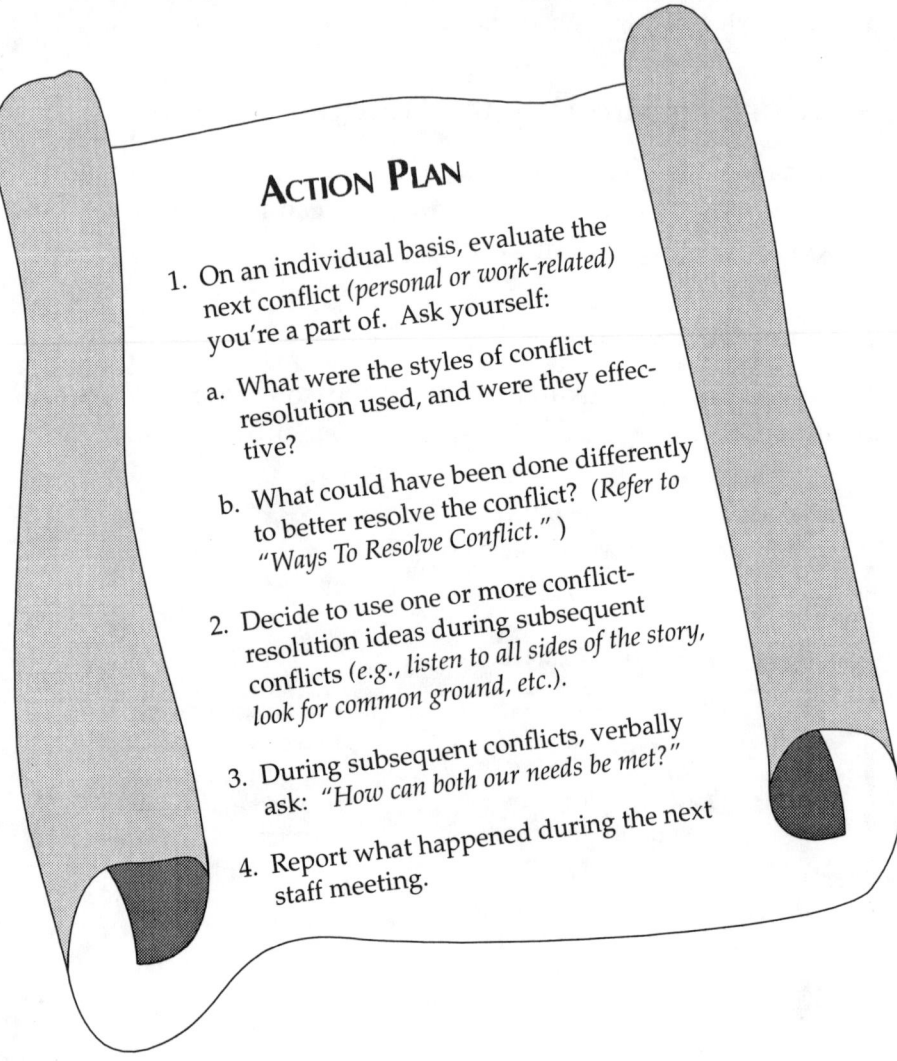

ACTION PLAN

1. On an individual basis, evaluate the next conflict *(personal or work-related)* you're a part of. Ask yourself:

    a. What were the styles of conflict resolution used, and were they effective?

    b. What could have been done differently to better resolve the conflict? *(Refer to "Ways To Resolve Conflict.")*

2. Decide to use one or more conflict-resolution ideas during subsequent conflicts *(e.g., listen to all sides of the story, look for common ground, etc.)*.

3. During subsequent conflicts, verbally ask: *"How can both our needs be met?"*

4. Report what happened during the next staff meeting.

Conflict resolution isn't simple, especially when cultural considerations come into play. But *"Diversity-Based Conflict Resolution"* can give your team or group practical tips to help successfully resolve workplace conflicts. It's a worthwhile investment if you use it.

CONFLICT RESOLUTION STYLES

"Avoidance" Style (I Lose—You Lose)

Avoidance is a lose-lose style, based on the saying, *"it is better to leave well enough alone."* Those who use this style may sidestep the issues, delay the issues, or repress their own feelings and needs.

"Competition" Style (I Win—You Lose)

Competition is a style where one person wins and one loses *(win-lose)*. It is based on the belief that *"might makes right."* People who use this style like to control situations and people. Often, this involves competition, and winning becomes an important goal.

"Adaptation" Style (I Lose—You Win)

Adaptation is a lose-win style that is based on the saying, *"You can catch more flies with honey than with vinegar."* Adapting may mean giving in to the other's wants, sacrificing your own goals, backing away from issues, and being too cooperative.

"Cooperation" Style (I Win—You Win)

Cooperation is a win-win style that is based on the belief that *"two heads are better than one."* This approach tries to find a way that meets each person's needs. Cooperation addresses the issues, explores the conflict situation, and finds creative alternatives to satisfy each person.

OBSERVER GUIDELINES

During The Roleplay

Your task is to observe what goes on in the role play.

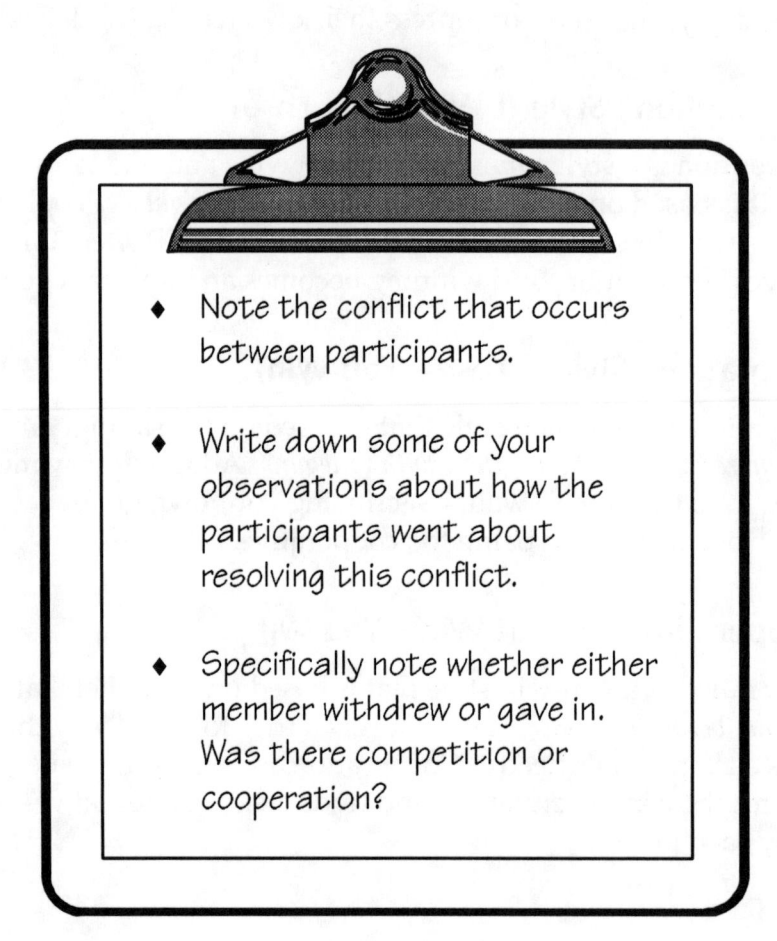

- Note the conflict that occurs between participants.

- Write down some of your observations about how the participants went about resolving this conflict.

- Specifically note whether either member withdrew or gave in. Was there competition or cooperation?

After The Roleplay

Your task is to report on the conflict that occurred and the way the pair resolved it.

Chapter Nine Worksheet: Overcoming Conflict

1. Which team or group in your organization could use *"Diversity-Based Conflict Resolution?"* Why?

2. Use *"Diversity-Based Conflict Resolution"* with your chosen team or group. Which style of conflict resolution was most prevalent? Which was least?

3. Which ways to resolve conflict did your team find most helpful? Why?

CHAPTER TEN

CROSS-CULTURAL COACHING

Coaching offers encouragement, promotes growth and development of employees, and helps them make a greater contribution to an organization. It can assist employees who may be encountering difficulty, yet still have strong potential to be more valuable to the organization. It can also help good employees become more productive in their current positions. Furthermore, coaching can empower an employee and show the organization's commitment to that person's success.

While coaching is a highly effective tool for employees in general, it is especially useful when dealing with employees who have not been part of the mainstream American work force. Organizations can show their commitment to valuing diversity by establishing a *"coaching climate"*—one in which personal and career growth of minorities, immigrants, and women can flourish.

Why Use *"Cross-Cultural Coaching"*

"Cross-Cultural Coaching" is designed to help individuals or groups understand the concept of coaching and to provide an opportunity to learn and practice the necessary skills. The role plays are culturally-based and offer insight into coaching employees with diverse cultural backgrounds. A commitment to coaching individuals from different backgrounds reveals a commitment to valuing diversity.

TOOLS FOR VALUING DIVERSITY

CROSS-CULTURAL COACHING

When To Use *"Cross-Cultural Coaching"*

Use *"Cross-Cultural Coaching"* when:

- You want your team or group to understand the importance of coaching.
- Your organization has a number of employees who are experiencing difficulty, yet clearly are valuable employees.
- You want to establish a work environment that values minorities, immigrants, and women.

Morice Azcarte, CEO of a manufacturing plant...

decided to use *"Cross-Cultural Coaching"* with his managerial team. The plant employed a number of minorities and immigrant workers, and Morice felt that the organization's success depended upon their success. *"This tool is exactly what we need,"* Morice commented to one of his managers. *"Next week we'll take a look at it."*...

How To Use *"Cross-Cultural Coaching"*

To use *"Cross-Cultural Coaching,"* complete the following five steps:

Step 1: Start the *"Cross-Cultural Coaching"* session

Step 2: Divide into pairs and discuss past coaching experiences

Step 3: Discuss the *"Coaching Plan"*

Step 4: Complete role play and small-group discussions

Step 5: Reconvene in large group and discuss

CROSS-CULTURAL COACHING

Step 1: Start the *"Cross-Cultural Coaching"* session

To start the session, complete the following:

> ◆ Provide a time limit. Generally, sixty to seventy-five minutes is sufficient.
>
> ◆ Describe the agenda to your group.
>
> ◆ Ask that they agree on a plan of action at the end of the session.
>
> ◆ Present a brief description of coaching, using the introduction to this chapter as your guide.

Point out to participants the following materials located at the end of the chapter, *"Coaching Plan,"* and *"Observer Guidelines."* Make copies of *"Cross-Cultural Coaching Role Plays"* from the Appendix. You will also need a pencil for each observer, and a flip chart and marker for yourself.

Morice talked to his team...
of managers, filling them in on the agenda and gaining their support for devising an action plan. *"We need to use coaching,"* Morice said, *"because we want our employees, all of them, to succeed."* He explained a bit more about coaching and was pleased to see that all eight of them appeared amenable to the idea....

Step 2: Divide into pairs and discuss past coaching experiences

Have your group members find a partner and ask them to discuss past experiences of having been coached or having coached others. They can draw from school, sports, and/or previous job experiences. Ask them which was more difficult—coaching or being coached, and why.

TOOLS FOR VALUING DIVERSITY

CROSS-CULTURAL COACHING

Point out to your team that many people feel coaching is often more difficult *(and yet more necessary)* when cultural factors need to be taken into consideration. Ask for their comments.

> ### *Morice grouped the team...*
> into pairs. *"Discuss any past experiences you have had with coaching. You might have been the coach or were coached. Think back to when you were in school or involved in a sport or even at your last job,"* he instructed. He gave the managers a few minutes to complete this portion of the exercise, because they seemed really involved in their discussions. Then he stopped them and asked them to share their experiences. Tsukasa, the human resources manager, thought it would be more difficult to coach than be coached. *"Being a coach requires a greater investment of time and effort,"* he said. Some of the others thought differently. All agreed that cultural factors would make the process more difficult....

Step 3: Discuss the *"Coaching Plan"*

Have each member of your group review the *"Coaching Plan"* and discuss the steps involved in coaching.

> ### *Morice referred to...*
> the *"Coaching Plan"* on page 100. *"Let's take a look at what's involved in the coaching process,"* he began, then continued by going through the information and asking for comments. *"I think Tsukasa was closer to the mark than the rest of us,"* Veda, the purchasing manager stated. *"Coaching is time-intensive."* Morice gave each of the other managers a chance to respond....

Step 4: Complete role play and small-group discussions

Divide your team members into groups of three and have each group choose who will be *"coach," "employee,"* and *"observer."* Point out to each observer the *"Observer Guidelines"* on page 101. Provide each coach and employee with a copy of *"Role Plays"* and assign them a single case.

CROSS-CULTURAL COACHING

Allow your team members an opportunity to read the descriptions of their respective roles. Then begin the role play, allowing about fifteen to twenty minutes. After the role play, have the observer lead the discussion, using his guidelines. Each person in the group is to talk about how he felt during the role play.

> *Morice divided the managers...*
> into groups of three. He joined Monsur, the production manager, and Veda. Morice volunteered to be the observer, Veda decided on the role of coach, and Monsur was the employee. Morice first distributed the handouts to each group member, then observed the role play in his group. After fifteen minutes, he called, *"Time,"* and asked the groups to start their discussions....

Step 5: Reconvene in large group and discuss

Ask your team members to rejoin the group and have each small group report on the results of the role plays. Explain that the skills of each coach have a strong influence on employee response and that when actually coaching an employee, it is important to plan ahead to best achieve the desired result.

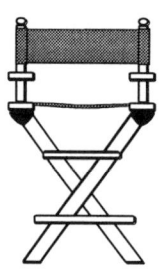

If time permits, have the group members exchange roles so that each person has an opportunity to play every part.

> *Morice led the managers...*
> in a discussion of the role plays. Most of the managers felt that the cultural differences made coaching a challenge. *"Coaching an American how to show individual initiative is different from coaching someone whose culture regards that trait as detrimental,"* Veda commented. *"I'm not saying it couldn't be done,"* she continued, *"but it would take more time and guidance."*
>
> Morice nodded. *"Does that make you less willing to coach individuals of different cultures?"* he asked. Veda thought for a moment. *"Not necessarily. It would just require more ingenuity, such as asking an employee who shows initiative to take the employee who needs coaching under her wing,"* she said. The other managers added their comments, and Morice wrote them on the flip chart....

CROSS-CULTURAL COACHING

Reinforcing The Lessons Learned

Can you come up with some concrete lessons you and your team have learned? *"Cross-Cultural Coaching"* is designed to help individuals realize how coaching can help improve an organization's work climate by increasing the acceptance and value of culturally-diverse individuals.

Lessons learned

List the lessons your team has learned.

> *Morice asked the managers...*
> to come up with a list of lessons they had learned from the role play and the discussions. They came up with the following:

LESSONS LEARNED

1. Coaching is sometimes essential for the development of employees, often more so with those of diverse backgrounds.

2. Effective coaching requires following a plan.

3. Coaching takes time, effort, and commitment.

Create an action plan

Once you've listed the lessons you have learned from *"Cross-Cultural Coaching,"* work with your team or group to create a plan that will help reinforce those lessons.

CROSS-CULTURAL COACHING

Morice looked carefully...

at each manager and said, *"Unless we can work on putting what we've learned to use, this session is a waste. So let's come up with an action plan."* The managers created the following action plan:

1. Choose an individual to coach.
2. Follow the steps in the coaching plan.
3. Report on the experience in three months.

Morice was pleased. *"I'm glad you're committed to coaching,"* he said. *"And I'll look forward to hearing the results. Let me know how your coaching situation is going and if I can be of any assistance."*

"Cross-Cultural Coaching" is one of the most comprehensive tools in this guidebook, because it requires an obvious investment of time and effort. But it also has a great potential payoff. Its use will increase the value of diversity in your organization.

CROSS-CULTURAL COACHING

Coaching Plan

Guidelines

- Mutually commit to the concept of coaching
- Acknowledge employee potential and show appreciation
- Elicit cooperation and encourage employee ideas
- Together, establish mutual goals and choose a course of action
- Provide positive reinforcement for improvement
- Hold periodic review meetings

Steps To Follow

1. Begin by explaining the process; describe your purpose in establishing a coaching relationship; and ask the employee to discuss what that person would like his/her future to be with the organization.

2. Tell the employee all the positive aspects of performance you have observed and express your satisfaction.

3. Explain how this is a joint effort and that cooperation is vital.

4. Discuss the employee's ideas and your own, and together select a course of action.

5. Offer constructive feedback as an ongoing process.

6. Hold periodic meetings to check progress, evaluate and adjust future action as applicable.

OBSERVER GUIDELINES

During The Roleplay

Your task is to observe what goes on in the role play and to look for the coaching skills that seem to be most effective. Write down some of your observations about the steps that the participants went through during this role play.

Specifically note how the employee responded and comment on the manager's ability to take on the role of coach in this situation.

After The Role Play

Your task is to lead a discussion in your small group based on the role play. Begin by giving feedback about what you observed.

After sharing your comments, ask the person who played the employee to discuss how she felt during the role play and to describe what was helpful and what wasn't. Have the *"employee"* comment on how she would have handled the situation if the roles had been reversed.

Ask the person playing the coach what seemed to work best and what was most frustrating. Have the *"coach"* comment on what he would do differently if given another chance.

CHAPTER TEN WORKSHEET: COMMITTED TO COACHING

1. Use *"Cross-Cultural Coaching"* with a team or group in your organization. What key lessons did you learn?

CROSS-CULTURAL COACHING

2. Do your team members see coaching as a viable option? Why or why not?

3. What plan of action did they create?

CHAPTER ELEVEN

SUMMARY

Workplace diversity is only a liability if you view it as such. Instead, see it through the lens of enlightenment and your view will be much sharper and more focused. Diversity in the workplace can become a valuable asset if you are willing to work at it *(and to make it work for your organization).*

This guidebook provides eight workable tools for valuing diversity. They aren't sure-fire formulas, nor are they secrets never before revealed. They are tools. And in the hands of willing and able users, they'll do a great job.

The key to their success is use. Use these tools, work with them, learn from them. Keep them on the shelf, and valuing diversity will remain an unreachable goal. Use them, refer to them, and you will see how diversity can strengthen an organization.

The challenge to value diversity is open. It will require stepping off the conventional path and walking into new territory. But considering the increasing amount of diversity in the workplace, it may be the only road to success. As the renowned American poet, Robert Frost, put it so well: *"Two paths diverged in a wood. And I—I chose the one less traveled by. And that has made all the difference."* Take the challenge to make a difference in your organization. Learn to value diversity!

APPENDIX

REPRODUCIBLE FORMS AND WORKSHEETS

Diversity-Based Team Building Role Assignments ... 108

Nonverbal Exchanges Exercise 111

Intercultural Communication Case Studies 112

Feedback Planner 116

Listening Competency: A Self-Assessment 117

Diversity-Based Conflict Resolution
Role-Play Situations 119

Cross-Cultural Coaching Role Plays 121

The pages in the Appendix are provided for you to photocopy and use appropriately.

APPENDIX

DIVERSITY-BASED TEAM BUILDING ROLE ASSIGNMENTS

A. The Loner

- ♦ You are basically independent and prefer working alone. You have found that you can succeed in this role and enjoy the recognition it brings. Individualism is your strong point.

- ♦ Being a group member is less important than the gratification that comes with accomplishment. You are a self-starter, respecting that characteristic in others, feel that your first responsibility is to yourself, and are unwilling to make sacrifices for the good of the group.

- ♦ On this project, you will try to divide up the tasks and have each group member be held responsible for one part of the entire project. You then plan to have it all come together at a later time.

Do not be too obvious, but try to influence the group to work independently. There is no assigned group leader.

B. The Belonger

- ♦ You like to work with others and feel that your first responsibility is to the group. You don't want to stand apart from them. Try to make sure that any decision is the result of total group agreement.

- ♦ You want the resulting work to represent a consensus expression of all the participants. You also feel certain that this project will reflect on the entire organization, and the group as a whole is accountable.

This activity has no leader. At the beginning, in a subtle way, attempt to sway the group to use consensus whenever possible.

C. The Go-Alonger

- You do not share the ambition and drive that motivates many people, and can't even understand those qualities in others. You will do whatever you can to avoid both risk and conflict.

- You prefer that all particulars are spelled out in any activity and you are uncomfortable working under pressure from others. Your response is always that you will go along with whatever they say.

- You worry a lot about maintaining your own personal comfort level, which is not tied to achievement.

This activity has no leader and you don't seem to care.

D. The Follower

- You would prefer having a strong leader who would tell you what to do. If the leader also enjoys special advantages, that's OK too. You do not like responsibility, but instead depend on a cooperating and passive role.

- You believe that a boss is always necessary and in this case you keep pointing out that the group needs a leader on this project. You would be happiest if someone took over the leadership of the group and you keep reminding the team about this.

Try to persuade others to take over the manager's role, but do it with subtlety.

APPENDIX

E. The Nurturing Member

- You need to have good relationships with your group above all else. You place less emphasis on individual performance than on group activity, avoiding competition within the group.

- You need a great deal of attention, always seeking smiles and approval from the group members. You want them to like you and compliment you and your contribution to the group.

F. The Pace Setter

- You are highly competitive and very ambitious. Harmony in the group is less important than addressing conflict. You have a habit of pressuring people to produce more. In any situation, you always want to win.

- You will try to have the males in the group take over, while discouraging the females. You have little patience with others who do not grasp things as quickly as you do.

Time is of the essence and you let the others know at every turn to get the task done, while still assuring the quality of the output.

G. The Observer

Tell the group that your role is only as an observer. In this role, you will not say or do anything.

Since there is no appointed leader, jot down notes on what you see happening and what type of leadership might be helpful in accomplishing the task more easily.

At the end of the activity, you will lead the group discussion, going over the various roles and the feelings of the participants. Encourage them to tell how they felt about their own roles and those of others in the group.

Nonverbal Exchanges Exercise

Pair A —Sender

In an open and receptive way, lead off the conversation by asking a question that calls for an explanation, such as: *"What's your favorite TV show or movie, and why?"* Now, cross your arms and legs and look away when the receiver answers you. In that same position make a positive response, while continuing to look away, being sure not to look at the receiver.

Pair A —Receiver

Simply answer the question you are asked.

Pair B —Sender

Stand up. Find out two new things about your partner while simultaneously moving closer and closer, breaking into the *"comfort zone"* of the person you are talking to.

Pair B —Receiver

Stand up and answer questions.

Pair C —Sender

Stand up. Say to the receiver in a normal tone with a smile, *"Come into my office."* Begin to walk away and then turn back around and repeat the same words, without smiling, and in an extremely harsh and demanding tone.

Pair C —Receiver

Stand up. Listen to what your partner says.

Pair D —Sender

Say to your partner the following statement: *"I really think we should get to work on this project."*

Pair D —Receiver

Say to your partner's comment with the following reply, *"Yes, I do too,"* but keep shaking your head in a manner that indicates *"no,"* while you're saying *"yes."*

APPENDIX

INTERCULTURAL COMMUNICATION CASE STUDIES

Case 1: Promotion Of Arthur Mitchell

You are a Team Leader and have been one for only a short while.

The majority of your team is white, although there are a significant number of African-Americans. Several weeks ago you promoted Arthur Mitchell to Lead Operator.

He's the first black ever promoted to that particular position in your department. This has caused some employee backlash including failure to promptly carry out work assignments. Aside from some negative department gossip, there have also been mock racist responses to his ordinary work requests. *("Yassir, Boss," for example.)*

You feel that this kind of behavior should not be tolerated.

Questions

♦ What do you think is causing these responses?

♦ Should you take some action?

♦ If not, explain why not.

♦ If so, describe the specific steps you will take.
  (If a memo is the decision, outline carefully, including all detail.)

APPENDIX

Case 2: Quick, Hide The Valuables

You are in a long line waiting to register for a technical course at a local college. The woman behind the desk seems to be dealing with the line efficiently so that it is moving along steadily.

When she looks up and sees the next person in line, she quickly moves her purse from the counter beside her to a shelf underneath the counter.

Questions

- What is the key issue here and how might it relate to diversity?

- If you were that next person in line, how would you feel and would you do anything?

- What about if you were a bystander?

Case 3: Who Has The Problem?

You have recently moved to the U.S.A. from central Mexico. You feel your English is quite good and are quite surprised when you notice that two of your team members speak to you louder than they do to anyone else, and certainly more slowly, even simplifying their language.

Questions

- What is the problem?

- How might the behavior of the two American-born team members be explained?

- How should you handle this situation?

APPENDIX

Case 4: The Big "Little Woman" Syndrome

You are a woman working for a male team leader who treats you very well, but you notice that he does not give you the same assignments as he gives the men. Instead, he offers you less challenging ones. In fact, he seems to feel protective.

The other day you overheard him on the phone talking to a female team leader who apparently was looking to have you transferred to her department. He was saying how good-looking you were and how sweet, but never how intelligent and capable, both which you are.

Questions

♦ Should you be concerned?

♦ If so, about what?

♦ Would you address your concerns? If not, why not?

♦ If so, what is the best approach to take?

Case 5: The Quiet One

A new employee from an Asian country was brought into the department. The staff felt that he was willing to take on any task and everyone was pleased. They saw him smile a lot, and heard him say to any request, *"Yes, I can do it."* He, too, appeared pleased and seemed to like his new position. One day, without notice, he left.

Questions

♦ Discuss the inferences and the absence of communication from all parties. What could have been done differently, so the end result might have been a happier situation?

Case 6: Selecting The Best Team Members

A group of male team leaders are getting together to set up a new project team. One of the people being considered is a woman and one of the men says that he heard that the woman being considered was pregnant. He stated that because the project was so important and very time-sensitive as well, he saw no reason to have a pregnant woman on the team.

Others, who had worked with the woman, all spoke about how effective she was and how important her contribution would be, even though she might have to miss some time. Nevertheless, the man who was objecting was adamant.

You are one of the members of the group who believes the woman should be used on the team.

Questions

- Whose problem is it?

- What do you think is going on here?

- Should you be concerned? If so, about what?

- Would you address your concerns? If not, why not? If so, what is the best approach to take?

APPENDIX

Feedback Planner

THE FEEDBACK PLANNER	
Name:	Date:
1. DESCRIBE CURRENT BEHAVIORS:	4. IDENTIFY ALTERNATIVE BEHAVIORS:
2. IDENTIFY SITUATIONS:	3. DESCRIBE IMPACTS AND CONSEQUENCES:

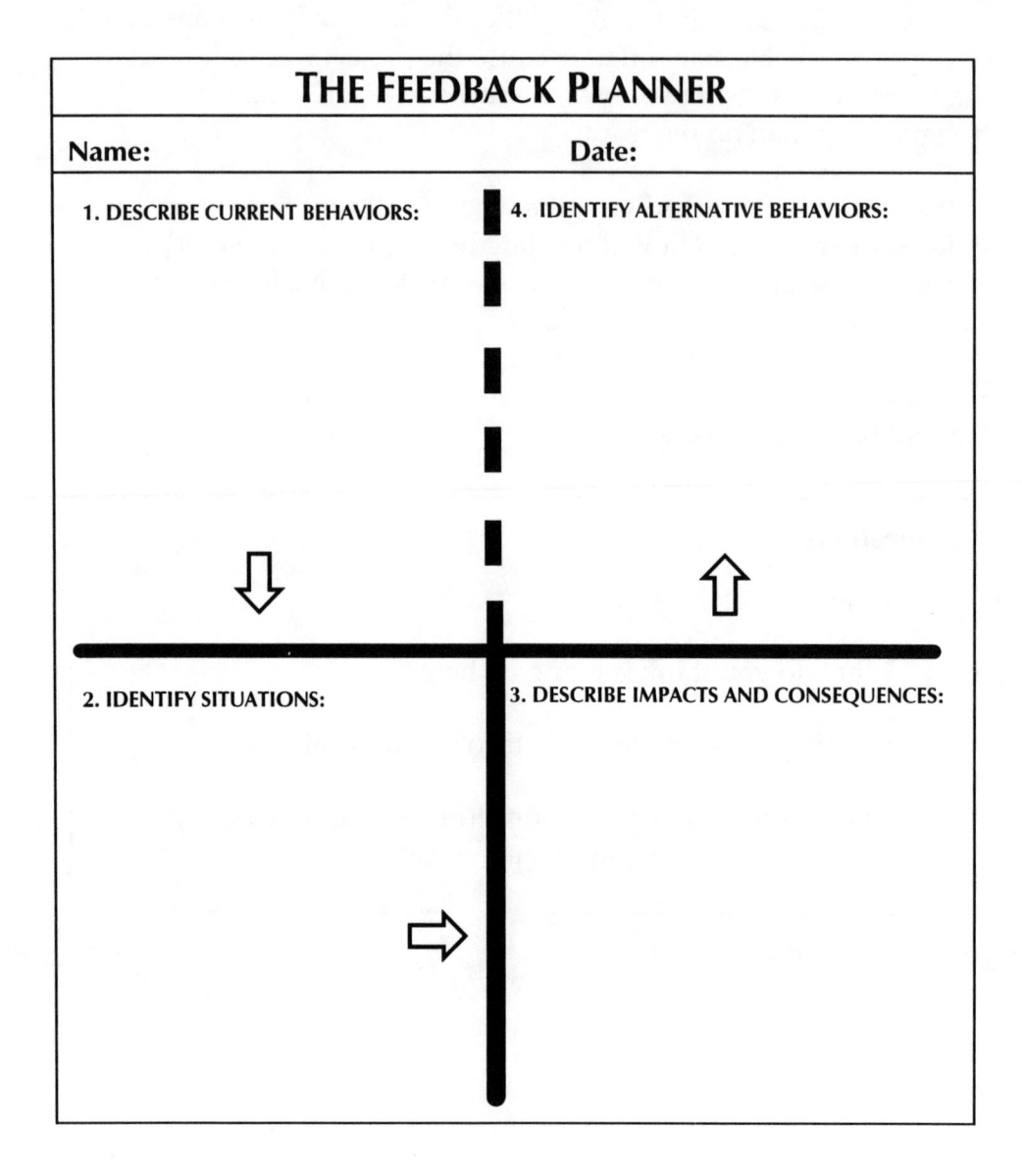

APPENDIX

LISTENING COMPETENCY: A SELF-ASSESSMENT

This self assessment can help you become more aware of your listening skills, determine where your strengths are, and discover what aspects you could develop more fully. Circle the number that represents your choice for each question.

Listening Competency	Almost Always	Frequently	Sometimes	Almost Never
1. Pay full attention to the speaker's message instead of what that person looks like?	4	3	2	1
2. Assume you know what the speaker will say and quickly start thinking of other things?	1	2	3	4
3. Listen carefully to others whose opinions are different than your own.	4	3	2	1
4. Make extra effort when you hear an accent?	4	3	2	1
5. Avoid listening if it will take extra effort to understand?	1	2	3	4
6. Listen without making judgments?	4	3	2	1
7. Let own emotions get in the way?	1	2	3	4
8. Make the speaker think you're giving your full attention even if you're thinking about other things?	1	2	3	4
9. Figure out and acknowledge the feelings that the speaker may be experiencing?	4	3	2	1
10. Attempt to determine the purpose of the communication *(the speaker's real needs)*?	4	3	2	1
11. Talk more than listen?	1	2	3	4
12. Become distracted easily by external sounds, people, or events?	1	2	3	4

TOOLS FOR VALUING DIVERSITY · REPRODUCIBLE FORM

APPENDIX

LISTENING COMPETENCY: A SELF-ASSESSMENT

Listening Competency	Almost Always	Frequently	Sometimes	Almost Never
13. Summarize in your own words what you heard the speaker say?	4	3	2	1
14. Turn your listening experience into a learning one, especially regarding differences in people, places and ideas?	4	3	2	1
15. Start thinking what you will say while the speaker is still talking?	1	2	3	4
16. Recognize your *"hot buttons"* and not let them get in the way of your listening?	4	3	2	1
17. Interrupt without giving the speaker opportunity to finish the thought?	1	2	3	4
18. Check assumptions about the message, the messenger, and the means of communication before you respond?	4	3	2	1

Scoring

Total the numbers in each category you have circled on the Self Assessment questionnaire to get your score.

Almost Always + Frequently + Sometimes + Almost Never = Total

_____ + _____ + _____ + _____ = _____

Super Listener	59-72
Better Than Average	46-58
Average	32-45
Needs Improvement	18-31

APPENDIX

DIVERSITY-BASED CONFLICT RESOLUTION ROLE-PLAY SITUATIONS

Situation 1— Participant "A":

Your company has moved to a new facility. There is one corner office with a window, which has new and modern furniture. You feel you should be given this office; unfortunately so does your coworker. In the organization, you are both at the same level. Your goal is to get that office.

Situation 1— Participant "B":

Your company has moved to a new facility. There is one corner office with a window, which has new and modern furniture. You feel you should be given this office; unfortunately so does your coworker. In the organization, you are both at the same level. Your goal is to get that office.

Situation 2— Participant "A":

Your organization is participating in a conference in Hawaii and there is one prepaid invitation for your department. There are two people who are equally qualified, of which you are one. You feel you should be given the opportunity to attend this conference. Unfortunately, so does your coworker. In the organization, you are both at the same level. Your goal is to go on that trip.

Situation 2— Participant "B":

Your organization is participating in a conference in Hawaii and there is one prepaid invitation for your department. There are two people who are equally qualified, of which you are one. You feel you should be given the opportunity to attend this conference. Unfortunately, so does your coworker. In the organization, you are both at the same level. Your goal is to go on that trip.

APPENDIX

Situation 3— Participant "A":

Your department has been budgeted money to hire one new staff member. You feel that this new employee should be assigned to you. Unfortunately, there is another person in your department who also feels that the new person should be assigned to him.

You are both at the same level and have equal power. Your goal is to get this new employee.

Situation 3— Participant "B":

Your department has been budgeted money to hire one new staff member. You feel that this new employee should be assigned to you. Unfortunately, there is another person in your department who also feels that the new person should be assigned to him.

You are both at the same level and have equal power. Your goal is to get this new employee.

CROSS-CULTURAL COACHING ROLE PLAYS

Time And Time Again

One employee from a culture different from your own is an excellent worker and willing to take on any task. However, he is considered a problem on the team because he is chronically late. He sees nothing wrong, insisting instead that he always completes his assignments and accomplishes more than many others.

You are annoyed because you and the others are usually on time, and on many occasions have to cover for him. You suspect that his difference in time sense may be cultural. You decide to try coaching him.

Boring, Booring, Boooring!

A woman who was born and raised in another country speaks English haltingly. However, she is an excellent assembler, truly dependable and very intelligent. In the assembly process, there is one very tedious job which she is frequently asked to do. Before she joined the team, this job was always rotated. She finds it boring and exhausting but is unwilling to complain as others did, and would never say *"no"* when asked to take it on. She finally tells you how she feels.

You are pleased that she felt open enough to come to you and decide you would like to help her. It appears that coaching would be the best way.

APPENDIX

CROSS-CULTURAL COACHING ROLE PLAYS

The Moonlighting Machinist

On your mostly young team, you have a much older machinist helper who moonlights as a machinist with another company. Your company brings in a new model machine that requires training, but the machinist helper is already familiar with this machine from his moonlighting job.

Still, the trainer assumes that, because of the helper's age, he will have a problem adapting to the new machine. The trainer publicly treats him as a slow learner and behaves in a very patronizing way.

You feel that coaching would help; who should be coached and how?

Ethnic Slurs

You are a white male team leader. Up to now, there have been no people of color on your team. You bring in a new member, an African-American male, whom you know to be a very hard worker.

On the first day, you hear one of your most competent team members say out loud, *"Hey, now that we're into diversity, there goes the neighborhood!"* By the end of the week, you have overheard that same person make several more insulting ethnic slurs directed towards the new member. You feel that coaching would help. How will you proceed?

Professional And Personal Development Publications From Richard Chang Associates, Inc.

Designed to support continuous learning, these highly targeted, integrated collections from Richard Chang Associates, Inc. (RCA) help individuals and organizations acquire the knowledge and skills needed to succeed in today's ever-changing workplace. Titles are available through RCA, Jossey-Bass, Inc., fine bookstores, and distributors internationally.

Practical Guidebook Collection

Quality Improvement Series
Continuous Process Improvement
Continuous Improvement Tools, Volume 1
Continuous Improvement Tools, Volume 2
Step-By-Step Problem Solving
Meetings That Work!
Improving Through Benchmarking
Succeeding As A Self-Managed Team
Measuring Organizational Improvement Impact
Process Reengineering In Action
Satisfying Internal Customers First!

Management Skills Series
Interviewing And Selecting High Performers
On-The-Job Orientation And Training
Coaching Through Effective Feedback
Expanding Leadership Impact
Mastering Change Management
Re-Creating Teams During Transitions
Planning Successful Employee Performance
Coaching For Peak Employee Performance
Evaluating Employee Performance

High Performance Team Series
Success Through Teamwork
Building A Dynamic Team
Measuring Team Performance
Team Decision-Making Techniques

High-Impact Training Series
Creating High-Impact Training
Identifying Targeted Training Needs
Mapping A Winning Training Approach
Producing High-Impact Learning Tools
Applying Successful Training Techniques
Measuring The Impact Of Training
Make Your Training Results Last

Workplace Diversity Series
Capitalizing On Workplace Diversity
Successful Staffing In A Diverse Workplace
Team Building For Diverse Work Groups
Communicating In A Diverse Workplace
Tools For Valuing Diversity

Personal Growth And Development Collection

Managing Your Career in a Changing Workplace
Unlocking Your Career Potential
Marketing Yourself and Your Career
Making Career Transitions
Memory Tips For The Forgetful

101 Stupid Things Collection

101 Stupid Things Trainers Do To Sabotage Success
101 Stupid Things Supervisors Do To Sabotage Success
101 Stupid Things Employees Do To Sabotage Success
101 Stupid Things Salespeople Do To Sabotage Success
101 Stupid Things Business Travelers Do To Sabotage Success

About Richard Chang Associates, Inc.

Richard Chang Associates, Inc. (RCA) is a multi-disciplinary organizational performance improvement firm. Since 1987, RCA has provided private and public sector clients around the world with the experience, expertise, and resources needed to build capability in such critical areas as process improvement, management development, project management, team performance, performance measurement, and facilitator training. RCA's comprehensive package of services, products, and publications reflect the firm's commitment to practical, innovative approaches and to the achievement of significant, measurable results.

RCA Resources Optimize Organizational Performance

Consulting — Using a broad range of skills, knowledge, and tools, RCA consultants assist clients in developing and implementing a wide range of performance improvement initiatives.

Training — Practical, "real world" training programs are designed with a "take initiative" emphasis. Options include off-the-shelf programs, customized programs, and public and on-site seminars.

Curriculum And Materials Development — A cost-effective and flexible alternative to internal staffing, RCA can custom-develop and/or customize content to meet both organizational objectives and specific program needs.

Video Production — RCA's award-winning, custom video productions provide employees with information in a consistent manner that achieves lasting impact.

Publications — The comprehensive and practical collection of publications from RCA supports organizational training initiatives and self-directed learning.

Packaged Programs — Designed for first-time and experienced trainers alike, these programs offer comprehensive, integrated materials (including selected Practical Guidebooks) that provide a wide range of flexible training options. Choose from:

- Meetings That Work! ToolPAK™
- Step-By-Step Problem Solving ToolKIT™
- Continuous Process Improvement Packaged Training Program
- Continuous Improvement Tools, Volume 1 ToolPAK™
- Continuous Improvement Tools, Volume 2 ToolPAK™
- High Involvement Teamwork™ Packaged Training Program

RICHARD CHANG ASSOCIATES

World Class Resources. World Class Results.℠

Richard Chang Associates, Inc.
Corporate Headquarters
15265 Alton Parkway, Suite 300, Irvine, California 92618 USA
(800) 756-8096 • (949) 727-7477 • Fax: (949) 727-7007
E-Mail: info@rca4results.com • www.richardchangassociates.com

U.S. Offices in Irvine and Atlanta • Licensees and Distributors Worldwide